Country Roads of

INDIANA

Drives, Day Trips, and
Weekend Excursions

Second Edition

Sally McKinney

COUNTRY ROADS PRESS

NTC/Contemporary Publishing Group

Library of Congress Cataloging-in-Publication Data

McKinney, Sally, 1933–
   Country roads of Indiana : drives, day trips, and weekend excursions /
Sally McKinney.—2nd ed.
      p.   cm.—(Country roads)
  Includes index.
  ISBN 1-56626-103-1
  1. Indiana—Guidebooks.   2. Automobile travel—Indiana—Guidebooks.
3. Rural roads—Indiana—Guidebooks.   I. Title.   II. Series.
F524.3.M38   1998
917.7204'43—dc21   98-30399
                                                   CIP

Cover design and interior design by Nick Panos
Cover illustration copyright © Todd L. W. Doney
Interior illustrations copyright © Barbara Kelley

Published by Country Roads Press
A division of NTC/Contemporary Publishing Group, Inc.
4255 West Touhy Avenue, Lincolnwood (Chicago), Illinois 60646-1975 U.S.A.
Copyright © 1999, 1993 by Sally McKinney
All rights reserved. No part of this book may be reproduced, stored in a retrieval
system, or transmitted in any form or by any means, electronic, mechanical,
photocopying, recording, or otherwise, without the prior permission of
NTC/Contemporary Publishing Group, Inc.
Printed in the United States of America
International Standard Book Number: 1-56626-103-1
99 00 01 02 03 04 ML 19 18 17 16 15 14 13 12 11 10 9 8 7 6 5 4 3 2 1

*This book is dedicated to the people of Indiana,
who can be wonderful hosts . . .
whenever they choose to be!*

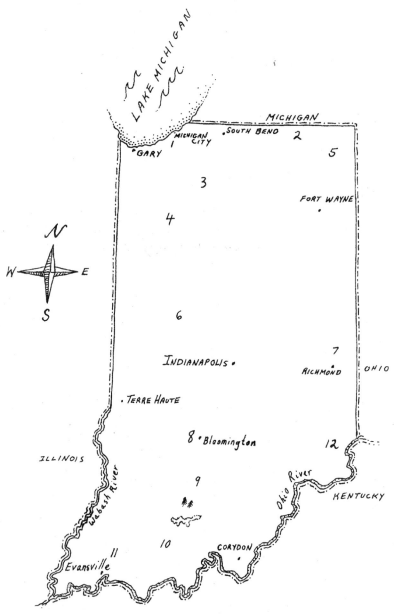

Indiana Country Roads
(Figures correspond with chapter numbers.)

Contents

Introduction

This travel guide will take you over a dozen routes— through some very interesting regions—and show you things to see and do along the way. From one country road, you can hire a canoe and paddle along scenic Sugar Creek—the way Indians once did—where cliffs create walls on either side. You'll glide on mirrored runs beneath red wooden bridges that resemble a hundred old calendar scenes. From another country road, you can visit Abraham Lincoln's boyhood haunts beside furrowed fields of corn. On still another country road, you'll discover a tiny airport where a pilot will waft you up over silver lakes rimmed with leafy trees.

To the uninitiated, the state named for Indians seems flat and unendowed. Yet Hoosiers in the know—and dedicated back-roads travelers—can find picture-postcard scenery beyond those cornfields.

More than five million people make Indiana their home, yet on some remote country roads, the only traffic may be a gridlock of horse-drawn buggies. The good people, natural beauty, and comfortable small towns that make Indiana a great state to visit also make it a fine place to live. Even if you've traveled far and wide, it's always good to come home to Indiana. From many a country road, the state flower, the peony, can be seen nodding hello on rural lawns. Each spring tulip trees (the official state tree) bloom along small-town streets. And now and then you're also likely to see the state bird, the cardinal, sitting on some fence post.

Located hundreds of miles from the nearest seacoast, Indiana stretches over roughly 36,000 square miles, including some 200 square miles of water. Meander across the northern third of the state to find factories, farmland, and fields. Dozens of sandy beaches rim Lake Michigan's shore, while hundreds of smaller lakes, scattered across the prairie, remain in the wake of Ice Age glaciers.

No less interesting is the rich, flat farmland of the central third, broken up by patches of woodland and all-American flag-waving towns. Follow a country road around two rural counties here to discover the greatest concentration of covered bridges in the nation.

In the southern region, you'll encounter rolling hills and forests still thick with virgin timber. Horses graze beside bubbling streams. Underground caves seem alive with their bright dripstone formations. Stroll along Main Street in a Hoosier river town and strangers greet you as friends.

For those who venture beyond the lights of Indianapolis, South Bend, and Evansville, there's still a lot of country in Indiana. Imagine hiking through sand dunes along a picturesque lakeshore. Fishing from a boat that glides past a nest of blue herons. Shopping in a quaint village perched on the banks of an early canal. Sipping hot cider at an autumn festival. Or squealing with the thrill of an old-time toboggan ride.

But the most vivid memories will come from encounters with people—the Amish schoolteacher, the village potter, the freckled kid who points the way back to town. Follow a country road into Indiana and memories of Hoosier people will follow you home.

1

From Courthouse to Lakeshore

Crown Point to La Porte

Getting there: From Indianapolis, take I-65 to U.S. 231; exit northwest to Crown Point. From the Chicago area, travel I-80/90 to Indiana and go south on I-65 to U.S. 231. U.S. 231 takes you into Crown Point.

Highlights: shop in a renovated courthouse; picnic, climb sand hills, or hike ancient Indian trails; relax in a country inn.

A leisurely drive through northwestern Indiana from Crown Point to La Porte lets you cruise through small-town America, beside small farms, through suburbs, along Lake Michigan's southern shore, and inland to Indiana's small-lake country.

Rolling into Crown Point you'll see wayside parks amid fields of corn give way to sturdy houses along tree-lined streets. Around the courthouse square at noon, people amble along sidewalks past a building topped with Victorian "wedding cake" decoration. Workers on lunch break line up to buy Polish sausage, and families picnic on the grass. For decades, in Hoosier county seats the town square has been a vital trading center. In Crown Point, it still is.

Crown Point's Lake County Courthouse, vintage 1878, is in the *National Register of Historic Places*. Ask the Crown Point Chamber of Commerce about its tours. City court still meets here, but the building mostly houses offices and shops. At Valentino's on the second floor, an old-time ice cream parlor, you can bite into spicy gourmet burgers then cool your palate with a fancy ice cream dish. The owners named the place for Rudolph Valentino, the silent-film star who got a marriage license here in 1923. During the 1920s, Crown Point became a "marriage mill" when celebrities like Red Grange, Ronald Reagan, Joe DiMaggio, and others got their licenses here with little waiting. Thirteen other shops in the renovated courthouse sell items ranging from stained glass to country gifts. Olivia's has gifts imported from 23 countries. Southwest Creations offers handicrafts brought from the cactus country, along with the artist-owner's own creations. In the past, Crown Point locals strolled around the courthouse square on Saturday nights. Nowadays, the best time to catch the downtown scene is between midmorning and late afternoon—any day but Sunday.

A block east of the courthouse square, on post office walls on the corner of East Street and Joliet Avenue, you'll see a mural by George Melville that shows the town's founder welcoming newcomers in the 1830s. Early settlers here traveled between small villages over sandy Indian trails flanked by swamps. Eventually the region attracted heavy industry. As Lake County grew, Crown Point was asked to merge with burgeoning cities to the north, but it never did. Good thing.

Walk over to 228 South Main Street to see a county jail that once held John Dillinger. While incarcerated here, the notorious Dillinger once used a hand-carved "revolver" stained with black shoe polish to take two hostages—and the county sheriff's car. He drove off with the hostages but (fortunately) was arrested again some weeks later.

Follow Joliet Avenue a little way east from the square, past St. Mary's Church, and you'll be on U.S. 231 south. You'll pass slow-moving vehicles, small trucks, and horse trailers as you drive through the countryside. At Stoney Run Farm with its stables and pastures, a lone white swan swims in a pond.

Following the signs, turn off for Stoney Run County Park, an easy drive of seven miles through gently rolling farmland. Stoney Run Creek meanders through a wide expanse of shaded lawns. At the park you can enjoy picnic shelters, a playground, a fishing pond, fitness and nature trails, and a Vietnam veterans' memorial. The day I visited, a young family was fishing beside tranquil blue-green water that mirrored the overhanging foliage. Rural Lake County is an appetizer meant to entice you into sampling more of Indiana's northwest region.

From Stoney Run County Park, return to U.S. 231 and drive east into Porter County. Hebron—not much more than a crossroads—has pleasant Victorian homes and a restaurant called Country Kitchen. In Hebron, you might want to make the short side trip to reach a cemetery used as a burial ground during the Civil War. To find it, follow Iowa Street south of U.S. 231 for three and a quarter miles.

Return to U.S. 231/SR 2 and continue north to Valparaiso. This is rolling countryside where white wooden fences crisscross small farms. Homes have been built scattered among the pines, and ducks ripple the surface of a pond.

On SR 2 just south of U.S. 30, Fetla's Bargain Center and Trading Post is a wonder of generic buildings crammed with hardware, toys, furniture, lawn ornaments, sporting goods, and boats. At one time Fetla's displayed brown bears in cages in the parking lot to get motorists' attention. Now they crowd the lot with stacked aluminum boats.

The name for Valparaiso, which is Spanish for "valley of paradise," was chosen by drunken sailors who had just come back from Chile. Over drinks in a local pub, everyone present agreed the name was a good one. Today most residents simply call it Valpo.

SR 2 continues north to Lincolnway, the main east-west thoroughfare in Valparaiso. This main street links Valparaiso University on "the Hill" with the courthouse square and its restaurants, shops, and offices. Drive along Lincolnway to find several possible eating places. Near the university, the Big Wheel drive-in, with a large, enclosed coffee shop, dates from the 1950s. The Spanish Don Quijote and Oneida's with "authentic Mexican food," also on Lincolnway, are nearer the square.

Follow Morgan Boulevard (also old SR 49) north out of Valparaiso past the old fairgrounds. Ignore the fast-food strip, and you'll soon be enjoying the low hills and small lakes to the north. Like other counties in Indiana's northwest, Porter County has become a network of towns, industries, and shopping strips held together by highways. Yet country roads remain, near patches of woodland, marshes, low sand hills, and lakes. Follow old SR 49 north and you'll see a lovely hillside golf course above Mink Lake, with its water lilies and reflections of late-day sun.

With car windows open, inhale the fresh breezes coming from Lake Michigan on the crest of each hill. Before air-conditioning, residents of Valpo would drive to the beaches just for the air. Take the SR 49 bypass then business route 49, and you'll be in Chesterton, where small craft shops and cafes form an "L" around the town park and an old wooden bandstand. SR 49 enters the village on Calumet Road, the one used by early settlers.

Chesterton was platted in 1852 by a man with a general store at the corner of Calumet Road and Broadway. The town grew after the Lake Shore & Michigan Southern Railroad came through. Thomas Centennial Park, where the band shell stands, was once the rail company's wood yard. Walk through the park and browse among the shops before heading north on Calumet Road past an old root beer stand. Even in these days of air-conditioning, indulgent parents still quench children's thirst with root beer on summer evenings.

Follow Calumet Road to Indian Boundary Line Road and on past Indian Oak Mall. Beyond the mall and behind some trees, the Gray Goose Inn occupies a rambling frame building beside a pond on a 400-acre site. Innkeepers Tim Wilk and Chuck Ramsey have decorated the inn with great personal style, so guests from around the world feel comfortable. Breakfasts are varied, featuring omelettes, muffins, and fresh fruit in season. The rich specialty coffee may give you a whiff of cinnamon. Take a second cup onto the sun porch—white wicker, dangling plants, antique canisters—to enjoy the woodland view.

Continue east on Indian Boundary Line Road and you'll return to SR 49, driving north to the dunes. Geologists say these sand hills were formed about 14,000 years ago. Glaciers helped form northern Indiana's chains of lakes, streams, marshes, bogs, and swamps. Ice Age winds spread shifting sands from the nearby dunes throughout the Kankakee Basin, and receding glaciers helped form rocky moraines. In this part of Indiana, early settlers rode through prairie grass that grew in marshy valleys. So tall was the grass, travelers said, that a man on horseback could tie the ends of grasses above his head.

Lake Michigan came from the Algonquian word *michi-gami*, meaning a large body of water. In 1809, an early traveler from Fort Wayne to Fort Dearborn (now Chicago) wrote that the Lake Michigan shore was "bounded by a mountain of sand, about one hundred feet high." He described northwest winds that acquired such force they could raise a cloud of sand that darkened the air. He saw sand mountains covered with stunted cedar and juniper trees and wrote of erosion and movement of the dunes, noting the way sand ridges receded as the water advanced.

Follow SR 49 north of Chesterton to the entrance of the Indiana Dunes State Park, a good place to explore the sand dunes. This 2,182-acre park was developed where Le Petit Fort once stood, built by the French in 1750. Though crowded during summer weekends, the park is a fascinating place to visit any time. You'll discover a sandy beach about three miles long and a 1,530-acre nature preserve. Depending on crowds, you may need to park a mile or more from the sand, bathhouse, pavilion, and picnic shelters. One of the marked, sandy hiking trails leads up to the park's tallest dune, Mount Tom, 192 feet above the beach. Follow other trails to the Big Blowout, an eroded, bowl-shaped depression, and the Pinery, a stand of virgin pines.

From the top of these great sand hills, you get a sweeping view of deep fresh water resembling an inland ocean. On a clear day, Chicago's skyline seems to rise from the water on your left. Straight ahead, the horizon divides the blues of the lake water from the paler sky.

Throughout the year the dunescape shifts and changes. In winter, with the water still too turbulent to freeze, the winds send great breakers crashing onto shore, and snowdrifts obscure the boarded windows of summer cottages. Even so, die-hard locals use the park for sledding and cross-country skiing. Melting snow and spring thaw give way to greenery and wildflowers. In spring, you'll be amazed to see great trees downed by winter storms and dead bushes uprooted by shifting sands. Yet the scrubby grasses still cling to the sandy ridges and down below, and mayapples flourish beneath the oaks.

Drive south to U.S. 12 and go 1.25 miles west and half a mile north to reach the Cowles Bog, a nature preserve. The first ethologist, Dr. Henry C. Cowles, studied plant succession in the dunes area at the turn of the century. Efforts to save the dunes began back in 1916 and eventually brought about the establishment of both Indiana Dunes State Park and Indiana Dunes National Lakeshore.

Head south of the bog on Mineral Springs Road for just over a mile and you'll find the Bailly Homestead, an early cemetery, and Chellberg Farm. A French-Canadian fur trader named Joseph Bailly built a trading post here to encourage settlement in 1822, and his descendants lived on the 42-acre homestead until 1918. Today, you can visit several early buildings still standing on the site.

Anders Chellberg, a Swedish immigrant, came after Bailly and built the farmhouse on the grounds in 1885. Visit Chellberg Farm in March to see maple syrup–making demonstrations at the annual festival.

Return to U.S. 12, and head west another six miles for the West Beach Visitors' Center at the Indiana Dunes National Lakeshore. The road you travel was once the Calumet Beach Trail, first used by Indians, then by pioneers between the Great Lakes and the Mississippi River. Note that sprawling sections of national lakeshore straddle the Indiana Dunes State Park. In all, the lakeshore contains 14,000 acres of dune land along Indiana's sandy Lake Michigan shore.

West Beach, a portion of Indiana Dunes National Lakeshore, offers free programs, hikes, exhibits, and other activities. From the visitors' center, hikers can walk along the various trails to explore miles of lowlands between sand ridges.

Drive east via U.S. 12 to reach other sections of the national lakeshore. Near the road you'll see Mount Baldy, a moving sand dune that rises 135 feet above the lake. Leave your car in the convenient parking lot and climb the shifting dune: if the winds are right, you'll hear the music of "singing sands."

Take U.S. 12 east, the Calumet Beach Trail, which rambles through pastoral Indiana countryside before reaching Michigan City. Divided into lots in 1832, the town grew up along Front Street where it met the old Michigan Road. Eventually the port and rail community did a big business shipping lumber and sand and manufacturing glass products. Turn left into Washington Park when you see the signs.

Since the 1970s, Lake Michigan has been stocked with trout, coho, and chinook salmon, and the fishing is terrific. Washington Park sports a fishing pier, a bathing beach, picnic areas, a band shell, and a zoo. Boats for lake cruises can be found at the marina. West of the bridge over Trail Creek, you'll spot an old (1858) lighthouse that once depended on a sperm-oil lantern that could be seen for 15 miles. Within the 90-acre lakeside park, you can hike a trail to the top of a sand dune and climb a 75-foot observation tower for a great panoramic view. Beyond the park, the old Hutchinson Mansion at 220 West Tenth Street has been turned into a charming bed-and-breakfast inn.

Exit Washington Park to the south and follow U.S. 12 and SR 39 toward La Porte. The drive goes by an old brewery covered with vines and a modest airport, and it slides beneath major highways before it again winds past woodland and farms.

La Porte grew along the Great Sauk Trail, later called the Old Chicago Road. To the early explorers and fur traders, La Porte (the gate) referred to an opening in the forest they used as a passage to the prairie. La Porte today is known for its lakes, and you'll drive beside two lakeside parks where willow trees spread dappled shade on the grassy shore. They're lovely places to stop if you're in need of a break.

Michigan City Lighthouse

Follow U.S. 35 into the city center and you can wrap up the drive. Stroll around La Porte County square with its courthouse built of Lake Superior sandstone. This hard-to-miss red building has distinctive gables and an enormous bell tower. At nearby Independence Plaza, a copper statue of a Potawatomi Indian holds a broken arrow, a monument to peace.

For More Information

All numbers are within area code 219.

Crown Point Chamber of Commerce: 663-1800

Lake County Convention and Visitors' Bureau (Merrillville): 980-1617 or 800-ALL-LAKE

Lake County Parks Department (24-hour phone line): 800-769-PARK

Indiana's Northcoast Charter Association, Inc. (fishing and boat trips in southern Lake Michigan): 800-231-6857

Don Quijote (Valparaiso): 462-7976

Porter County Convention and Visitors' Bureau (Chesterton): 926-2255 or 800-283-TOUR

Gray Goose Inn (Chesterton): 926-5781

Mary's Ice Cream Parlor and Restaurant (Chesterton): 926-3894

Indiana Dunes State Park (office; Chesterton): 926-1952

Indiana Dunes National Lakeshore (Porter): 926-7561

Parks and Recreation (Michigan City): 873-1506

Port Authority (Michigan City): 872-1712

Hutchinson Mansion Inn (Michigan City): 879-1700

La Porte County Convention and Visitors' Bureau (La Porte): 872-5055 or 800-634-2650

2

Meander Through Amish Country

Elkhart to Lagrange

Getting there: From the Chicago area, drive east on I-80/90 to Indiana, and exit at SR 19. Drive south to Elkhart. From the Detroit area, head south on I-75, then west on I-80/90. Exit at SR 19 and drive south to Elkhart.

Highlights: stroll through city parks and a vintage small town; shop for handicrafts; visit an Amish family or bike past Amish farms; sample country-cooked food.

For a drive in the slow lane, travel through Indiana's Amish country with its tidy farms, clanging school bells, and horse-drawn buggies. In two northern counties, Elkhart and Lagrange, about 17,000 Amish live in one of the three major communities in rural America.

The gateway to Indiana's Amish country is the city of Elkhart, named for an island at the junction of two rivers.

Early Indians thought an island where the
Elkhart River met the St. Joseph River was
shaped like an elk's heart. Later, the island
became known as Coeur de Cerf to the
French. When one pioneer traveler
through Indiana visited this place, he
wrote in his journal, "Here is a place formed
by nature for a town." Over the years, Elkhart
has become a town indeed, a manufacturing center known for
musical instruments, recreational vehicles, and pharmaceuti-
cals (Miles Laboratories, Inc.).

Stroll along the paths in Elkhart's lovely riverside parks
and you'll see how the Big and Little Elkhart Rivers feed and
nourish this region. In the surrounding community Amish,
Mennonites, and "English" (the term the Amish use for everyone else) live and work side by side.

The Elkhart County Tourism office has a map of one bicycle route through Elkhart's riverside parks and five bike routes
through Amish Country small towns and past B&Bs. Two
routes are more than 20 miles long, but the map also shows
shorter loops—the routes all connect. Ask, too, about the
Heritage Trail Audio Tapes; the office will lend one with a $10
deposit.

One favorite walk in Elkhart starts at Jackson Boulevard
and runs north and east along the Elkhart River. A footbridge
leads over the water to the historic island. From there, you
can cross the 270-foot Miles Centennial Foot Bridge that spans
the wider St. Joseph River and leads into Pulaski Park, the site
of Elkhart's first post office.

Stroll west along Beardsley Avenue and you'll pass beside
the luxurious mansion called Ruthmere. Once the home of
Albert and Elizabeth Beardsley, the residence was named for a
child who died in infancy. The 1910 structure, open to the public as a memorial, has been elaborately restored. Within the
building, a blend of beaux arts and prairie school architecture, you'll find hand-painted decor, polished wood panels,

velvet murals, Tiffany lamps, and the lavish use of silk, satin, and brocade.

Continue walking west on Beardsley Avenue two more blocks to see the home of the town's founder. The Beardsley home is on Main Street, Elkhart's tree-lined central thoroughfare. Albert Beardsley's uncle, Dr. Havilah Beardsley, built this two-story brick home and also operated the town's first sawmill.

Also in Elkhart, the S. Ray Miller Auto Museum at 2130 Middlebury Street displays antique cars along with mannequins wearing vintage clothing.

When you've tired of walking, retrieve your car and follow Main Street south to Jackson Boulevard, which is also SR 120 east. Drive east from Elkhart toward the town of Bristol. You'll pass well-kept homes built early in the century and a riverside park with grassy lawns, a river walk, and stately year-round homes. Beyond, SR 120 enters open country where fields of lavender and white flowers bloom in spring.

The town of Bristol occupies a bank of the Little Elkhart River upstream from Elkhart. On or near Vistula Street (SR 120) you can see many of the community's historic buildings: an old opera house, restored early homes that are still being used, and a lovely white clapboard church. Bristol, they say, was first settled by northeast Yankee farmers. At 110 East Vistula, there's an "old store"—a warehouse built by an early grain merchant. Two blocks south of Vistula at the corner of Charles and Joseph Streets stands a Greek Revival home built by a partner in a milling operation. The Bristol Opera House, at 212 East Vistula Street, opened in 1897 and served as a venue for many traveling entertainers. St. John of the Cross Episcopal Church, at 601 East Vistula, built in 1851, is held together by wooden pegs.

Follow SR 15 south of Bristol through horse-farm country. You'll pass an old brick home called Colonial Ridge, covered with vines. At Elkhart Avenue (CR 8), head east to Bonneyville Mill County Park. In this 222-acre river preserve you'll find picnic shelters, nature trails, playgrounds, fishing, and an observation tower to climb. Edward Bonney built the dam and the water-powered mill in 1832. At the gristmill—the oldest one in Indiana in continuous operation—between May and October see stone-ground flour made from corn, wheat, buckwheat, or rye, and buy some to take back home. In winter, the Bonneyville Mill looks lovely against new-fallen snow, and the park is used for sledding or cross-country skiing.

After exploring the park, return west on CR 8 to SR 15. Turn left and go south on SR 15 toward Goshen for a winding drive past apple orchards, farm markets, and old red barns. Bucolic white-faced cattle graze in the fields, and the countryside seems lush and nurturing.

Named for the biblical land, Goshen sits in a fertile prairie and has become a manufacturing and trading center, especially for the Mennonites and Amish. In central Goshen, where SR 15 meets SR 4, you'll find two-story businesses and shops clustered along Main Street. Old brick streets lead from the center of town, and scattered willows arch gracefully beside the Elkhart River.

The Old Bag Factory, a restored 1890s building at 1100 Chicago Avenue on the corner of Indiana Street, houses a complex of shops and the studios of craftspeople. Browse among the custom hardwood furniture, pottery, candles, jewelry, sculpture, bakery goods, and handmade quilt shops, then relax in the tearoom. It is open between 9:00 A.M. and 5:00 P.M. on weekdays, with shorter hours on Saturday. As with many businesses here, the Old Bag Factory is closed on Sunday.

From Goshen, head southwest on SR 119 toward Nappanee. You'll share the road with horse trailers, old cars, and an occasional vintage pickup piled high with hay bales. You'll drive beside pine groves, windmills, and fields of wildflowers. On one farm, a horse stands harnessed to a buggy in the driveway while a woman in a sun-bleached dress hoes weeds in garden rows.

Turn left when you reach SR 19, and drive south to Nappanee, a community named for a Canadian town with a gristmill. The Canadian town got its name from *napani*, a tribal word for flour. When the railroad came into Elkhart County, the Hoosier town became a shipping center for furniture, canned goods, and (of course) flour.

Well-publicized Amish Acres, at 1600 West Market Street in Nappanee, consists of historic Amish buildings brought from other sites and newer buildings providing visitors' services. The resulting 80-acre tourist farm functions as a living history museum. You can watch women making quilts, cooking, making candles—in short, going about traditional everyday tasks. Farmers plow fields with teams of horses. In season, maple syrup, apple cider, and other foods are made. The Restaurant Barn at Amish Acres serves hearty farm-style meals to hordes of diners. While you're there, take in a performance of the long-running *Plain and Fancy* or one of the classic musicals—all suitable for the family.

In Nappanee, Coppes Street Cabinet Manufacturers and the Borkholder Country Furniture Store are known for fine hand-crafted furniture. At Dutch Village, craft and antique shops, a bakery, a soda fountain, and an auction await you. Horses pulling buggies clip-clop along the streets during the day, and farm workers balance shopping bags on bicycles. Head east from Nappanee on U.S. 6, and be alert for horses and buggies. They usually sport Elkhart County license plates and "slow-moving vehicle" signs. At roadside stands along the way, you might see houseplants, flowers, vegetables, and local honey for sale.

Leave U.S. 6, turning north onto SR 15 toward Goshen. As you drive along the railroad tracks, you'll get a good look at small-town rural America: tiny New Paris—where the World Mission Press has its headquarters—and Waterford Mills.

Back in Goshen, note the South Side Food Shop with its art deco facade. Follow SR 15 past the Goshen College campus, a four-year liberal arts school still owned by the Mennonite Church. About two-thirds of today's students belong to the Mennonite faith. To promote international awareness and understanding, Goshen College requires all students to live for a while in another country.

At the Elkhart County Courthouse in downtown Goshen, link up with SR 4 and head east out of town. In summer, Little League players may be tossing and hitting balls. In winter, snowmobilers could be crossing the snow-covered fields. Year-round, you can see Amish farm homes, painted white, without the wires usually strung between farm buildings. Lacking automatic clothes dryers, Amish women hang clothes outside to dry. Lacking a power lawn mower, an older child provides the muscle power that turns lawn-mower blades. When I drove through here, young women walked beside the road, their hair held back by bonnets, pushing two babies in a handmade cart.

What a contrast, then, to visit the Checkerberry Inn, just south of SR 4 on CR 37, set in a 100-acre private estate. A long front porch overlooks a flat lawn where guests compete on the croquet field. Each of the 12 rooms has been individually decorated. The Checkerberry Inn has a reputation for fine food, special beer and wine tastings, and hot-air balloon events; note that it closes in winter.

SR 4 ends at SR 13, so turn left and go north on SR 13 to Middlebury in the heart of Crystal Valley. Sunlight filtered by sheer clouds above the rural landscape gives the region a luminous beauty. Beside the road you'll see a log cabin and sheep grazing in a stubbled field. Beside a garden, a man and woman stand as if they were an artist's models in peasant clothing.

SR 13 runs on north through dairy country into Middlebury. You'll enter the town on South Main Street. A tiny creek, now dry, once ran through the small park in the town center.

You can sometimes see a horse and buggy hitched to a rail outside the Dairy Queen. Take CR 16 east of Middlebury past a shady public park, and you'll find a two-lane blacktop road leading into the heart of Crystal Valley.

Frugal and conservative because of their beliefs, Amish farmers may supplement their incomes with businesses on the side, such as repairing buggies, sharpening tools, or making cabinets. You'll see many of these entrepreneurs' modest signs in Crystal Valley.

Travel east of Middlebury on a late spring evening, and you could well see one buggy after another clip-clopping along the road. In one, an elderly couple moves somberly toward the cemetery. In another, a young man heads over the hill. On one balmy evening, more than half a dozen buggies rolled through the valley while the hollow clopping of horses' hooves echoed from the hills.

On CR 16 about three miles east of Middlebury, the Deutsch Kase Haus makes and sells cheese. Through a wide glassed-in window, you can watch each step in the cheese-making process. Continuing east, you'll eventually reach Shipshewana, known to locals as Shipshe. This bustling small town with its grain elevator has a group of craft, antique, and gift shops arranged along a grid of streets between Van Buren and Morton in the central part of town.

At the Blue Gate Restaurant, named for an early gristmill, you dine on Amish and Mennonite cooking. Across the street, Riegsecker's Marketplace has dozens of shops selling hand-made quilts, country art, wall hangings, lace, stained glass, dolls, and copper pieces. The Buggy Wheel Restaurant, next to the Morton Street Bed and Breakfast, has its own bakery. The Old Davis Hotel, near the railroad, dates from 1891. The Beecher House, built the same year, has become a gift shop.

"Junque" store junkies come to Shipshewana for its vast outdoor flea market (south of town, east of SR 5). Here more than a thousand vendors sell everything from baby chicks to picture frames. Vehicles can sometimes park near the downtown shopping area, but flea-market stalls, set on loose gravel, can only be reached on foot. In any case, wear sturdy walking shoes.

After wandering about the flea market, you might "set a spell" with the locals in the livestock auction barn, between the downtown and the flea market. While you watch from the benches, an auctioneer calls out bids for cattle, hogs, and other livestock as they are driven through a muddy, fenced enclosure to be viewed by prospective buyers. At the first such auction in Shipshewana in 1922, six pigs, seven cows, and several head of young cattle were sold. Today, a variety of antiques, livestock, horses, and carriages are auctioned on different days according to a regular schedule.

South of Shipshewana and west of the vast flea market, the Menno-Hof (Mennonite-Amish) Center relates the history of religious persecution and migration. Centuries ago, many early Christians left Europe for the New World in search of religious freedom. Today, the worldwide communities of Amish and Mennonites number about 750,000 living in 57 different countries.

The nonprofit Menno-Hof facility was built in traditional Amish fashion with a crew of perhaps 200 volunteers. The barnlike structure, made of rough-hewn oak beams, was made using knee braces and wooden pegs. Exhibits include a European courtyard, a cobblestone street, a dungeon, the hold of a sailing ship, and a traditional meetinghouse—all dramatic history.

From the Menno-Hof Center, turn onto CR 250 north, the street south of the vast flea market, and follow this paved road to CR 200 north. The CR 200 route east toward Lagrange can be a delightful ride, for the country road rambles through pastoral Crystal Valley with its rolling hills. Pedal up gentle rises, and then coast down the eastern slopes among the Amish farms, gardens, and fields. On summer evenings,

Amish teenagers also pedal bicycles to volleyball games or gatherings of friends. Teens don't have their own buggies yet, and they certainly don't have cars. A pile of bicycles under a tree usually means there are teenagers nearby.

In autumn, school bells clang throughout the valley, calling children to two-room Amish schools. A schoolteacher may alternate classroom sessions with doing chores on the family farm. Wearing plain clothing, no makeup, and sturdy shoes, two teachers may supervise 36 children in grades one through eight. One teacher claimed she enjoys teaching, believes in discipline, and said, "I think children reflect what you are." As she rang the school bell, the sound reverberated to the hills.

Although you may be restless to complete a drive through Amish country, it takes patience to slow down—yet again—for the buggy ahead. Eventually, the driver in a dark hat and the woman in a bonnet may turn onto a gravel road before disappearing in dust beyond the hill. Keep driving along CR 200 north, and you'll complete this Amish country adventure at SR 9 north of Lagrange. The rural landscape and the close ties of people to the land, is a heritage we all share. The displays in the Menno-Hof Center come back to mind:

"What we sow, that we shall also reap."

"Food is a gift of God to be enjoyed, and shared with those who are hungry."

"A car may get you there quicker. But in a buggy you see and hear things along the way."

For More Information

All numbers are within area code 219.

Elkhart County Convention and Visitors' Bureau (Elkhart WalkTour map; Elkhart): 262-8161 or 800-262-8161

Ruthmere Museum (Elkhart): 264-0330

S. Ray Miller Auto Museum (Elkhart): 522-0539

Bristol Opera House (Elkhart Civic Theater; Bristol): 848-4116

Elkhart County Parks and Recreation Department (Goshen):
   535-6458

The Old Bag Factory (Goshen): 534-2502 or 800-531-2502

Amish Acres, Inc. (Nappanee): 773-4188 or 800-800-4942

The Checkerberry Inn (Goshen): 642-4445

Das Dutchman Essenhaus (Middlebury): 825-9471

Menno-Hof Center (Shipshewana): 768-4117

Shipshewana Auction and Flea Market (Shipshewana): 768-4129

Lagrange County Convention and Visitors' Bureau (Lagrange):
   463-8090

3

Wings Across the Plains

Jasper–Pulaski Fish & Wildlife Area
to Plymouth

Getting there: From Indianapolis, take I-65 and exit at SR 24; travel east to Reynolds. Drive north on U.S. 421 to Jasper-Pulaski Fish & Wildlife Area. From the Chicago area, take I-80/90 to I-65 south. Exit at SR 2, go east to U.S. 421, then drive south to Jasper-Pulaski Fish & Wildlife Area.

Highlights: view masses of sandhill cranes, take a nature walk, or pick berries; dine beside a lake or rent a boat; visit an Indian memorial.

You could well start this drive across Indiana's sandy fields, marshy plains, and glacial lakes with a visit to the Jasper-Pulaski Fish & Wildlife Area. Imagine yourself hidden in the marshes just before dawn, where you can feel the chill of autumn and hear the primeval squawking of several thousand birds. At first light, you can make out their grayish oval bodies as they stand on spindly legs in marshy* grass. As their cries become louder, and as if on some pre-arranged signal, the masses of birds take flight, scattering across a wan sky but soon becoming marvelously organized in winged formations. . . .

The entrance to the reserve is a mile and a half west of U.S. 421 on SR 143. Sign in at the designated area and pick up a free Jasper-Pulaski Fish & Wildlife Area map; you'll find an array of activities available. Beyond the entrance is a grassy picnic area and playground shaded by hardwoods and pines. If you're here to see the cranes and migrating Canada geese, find the observation towers on the map. The nearest tower, across CR 1650, is a short walk from the entrance. Note that the activities allowed at Jasper-Pulaski are many and varied. In season, hunters wander about looking for prey, and at other times, they come for target practice. For your own safety, be sure to sign in and then study the coded map, find the right area for the activity you choose, and follow instructions posted for safety.

Sandhill cranes, the Jasper-Pulaski area's star visitors, stand up to three and a half feet tall, weigh 10 to 12 pounds, and fly on wingspreads up to seven feet. During the autumn, they leave nesting grounds in the wetlands of southern Canada and the upper Midwest, using the Jasper-Pulaski area as a refuge before flying to marshlands in southern Georgia and Florida for the winter. During the spring, some cranes also stop at Jasper-Pulaski on the way to their summer habitats.

Cranes used to inhabit northern Indiana in greater numbers, but much of their wetland habitat has been drained for farmland and homes. Now protected by state and federal laws, the sandhill cranes find a safe haven at Jasper-Pulaski. They roost in wetlands at night and feed in farmers' fields by day. The best times to see them here are at dawn, just before they leave to feed in the fields, and at dusk, when they come back to the wetland to roost.

The cranes eat berries, roots, insects, frogs, small animals, and waste grains, as well as the young, tender shoots of corn and wheat in the spring.

There are 8,022 acres of wetland and upland game habitats in the Jasper-Pulaski Fish & Wildlife Area, along with 2,000 acres of wetlands. Because of this habitat, increasing numbers of the once-endangered sandhill cranes have been stopping during spring and fall migrations. Now birdwatchers as well as hunters and fishermen come to Jasper-Pulaski during various seasons.

In prehistoric times, melting glaciers and westerly winds scattered sand across these plains, forming dunes and depressions. When no one is hunting there, you might want to walk through the Tefft Savanna Nature Preserve, a 480-acre portion of the Jasper-Pulaski Fish & Wildlife Area located to the west of CR 400 east (refer to the handout map you picked up at the sign-in area). Established in 1980, this preserve shows what much of the area looked like when settlers first came. More than 260 types of plants have been found in the preserve, with about 30 of them rare, threatened, or endangered. There are also more than a hundred species of birds in the Tefft Savanna, plus scattered trees, low bushes, gophers, snakes, butterflies, katydids, and leafhoppers.

One of the best ways to observe the birds and other wildlife at the Jasper-Pulaski area is along the Observation Trail, a gravel road that winds between marshes and ponds. Here willows blow in the wind, and water lilies glide on the water's surface. Some visitors park in the lot here to go fishing in gravel-pit ponds, even in winter. The network of roads shown on the Jasper-Pulaski map allows visitors to leave the reserve by various routes.

Drive on CR 700 north and you'll meet U.S. 421. Turn left on U.S. 421 and drive north, and you'll see a sign for Blue Acres Farms, famous for blueberries. At the corner of SR 10, you'll also find directions to Spenner's Strawberry Farm. In season, the sun-ripened berries are so sweet you won't even need sugar.

SR 10 east toward North Judson runs straight as a gunshot through rural flatlands. People here live in modest homes scattered along the roadway, and the social life revolves around churches—or roadside taverns. Occasionally, you'll see sandy ridges and marshy ponds, remnants of the vast prairies where native tribes once roamed.

Pass through North Judson and continue on to Bass Lake, where SR 10 rims the lake's southeastern shore. If you stay on the lakeside road, you can circle the lake and join SR 10 again, where you left it, to drive east to Culver. Unlike the roads around other natural lakes found in the northern part of Indiana, this public road runs between the lakeside cottages and the shore. For a change, you get a really good look at all the water activities while you drive the 11-mile route.

In the early 1900s, Bass Lake drew many fishermen. Summer people from Chicago and northern Indiana stayed in hotels and cottages along the shore. The lake at that time was surrounded by marshes, making roads impractical. The Bass Lake State Beach House was built in the 1930s. Holiday-makers came in on the Erie Railroad and got off the train at Bass Station. Some cottages still standing now were built during that time. Drive around Bass Lake today and you'll see Bass Lake State Beach, where you can sunbathe, swim, picnic, or sit back against a shade tree near the beach just to relax. Down the road from the beach is a sign for bicycle rentals and a place where you can rent a rowboat.

The Bass Lake State Fish Hatchery, which was established in 1912, is also located near the beach. Although it no longer stocks fish, it's interesting to walk about the grounds.

At the Shore Club, near Bass Lake's North Beach on the circle drive, you can dine on steaks, seafood, or appetizers or on homemade pizza and sandwiches. A complete dinner with appetizer, main course, and dessert comes to less than $20. Sip an Irish Summer Coffee in a padded booth in the bar and you can watch the late-day sun glow behind the lake. The Shore Club's Sunday brunch attracts people from miles around. Once a year, at the Bass Lake Festival, people join in sing-alongs, water volleyball games, and raft races. In fact, there are so many activities that people who come here to get away from it all can't get away at all.

For less congestion, take U.S. 35 south to Tippecanoe River State Park. Enter on the east side of the highway south of Beardstown. Tippecanoe Park flanks a beautiful stretch of river, great for paddling a canoe or watching scenery. If you get the urge to camp out but didn't bring camping equipment, ask about the Rent-a-Tent area. There are also bridle trails and bicycle rentals available.

When you leave, return via U.S. 35 north to Bass Lake and take SR 10 east to Culver. You'll pass the entrance to the Culver Military Academy, a coeducational private school with a collegelike campus. Since the school first opened in 1894, the buildings have spread over a lush, 1,500-acre site beside Lake Maxinkuckee. The Culver Military Academy Historic District has several historic buildings you can visit. Stroll around the wooded campus and you'll see the striking Culver Memorial Chapel with its 156-foot Tudor-Gothic tower. The building's radiant stained-glass windows were handcrafted in England.

Each summer more than 1,400 of Culver's young people sign up for a program centering around water sports, horsemanship, wood crafts, and Indian lore. On Sunday evenings, you can watch parades. On Saturday nights students perform authentic Indian dances.

From the academy, drive east of Culver via SR 10 to SR 117, turn south, and drive along the lake to the Culver Marina at 3000 East Shore Drive. There, the showroom office

staff handles boat rentals, and if you don't know how to operate a boat they'll show you how. Out on the lake, you can see
ducks swimming and, at times, watch the fish wiggle through
the clear, shallow water. If you like, anchor at the park across
the way and go for a swim. Phone ahead to reserve a boat
before you arrive.

After cruising around Lake Max for a while, head south
on SR 117. At SR 110, turn west. Travel west to SR 17, turn
right, and head north along the lake's west side. When you
reach the turnoff at Seventeenth C Road, go east toward the
lake, and you'll segue into Main Street and Lake Shore Drive.
In the heart of Culver, you'll find an old movie theater, a
restaurant, a tiny donut shop, and others beside the lake. This
is a walkable town. Saunter past the old Kreuzberger Saloon at
303 State Street, built in 1894 and now a private residence.
The building once housed a pub, sleeping rooms, and a bowling alley. The Woodbank Summer Cottage at 2738 East Shore
Lane, on the lake, has made the *National Register of Historic
Places*.

After your stroll, drive north on Lake Shore Drive. The street
intersects SR 10 at the stoplight, where you pick up SR 17. As
you head north on SR 17, don't miss the intriguing country
store on the right. Country auctions are sometimes held opposite the store. Proceed north on SR 17, and you'll come to
Burr-Oak, a wide spot in the road with an antique shop open
six days a week. Continue north on SR 17 over the murky,
brownish Yellow River. The Marshall County Memorial
Forest is on the right. Along the way, you'll see an odd house
built of tiny pieces of stone.

Continue north to the road for Twin Lakes. Turn right and
drive east at the sign; eventually, you'll learn this is West
Twelfth Road. At Twin Lakes, a little crossroads store sells
fishing licenses, ice, and other supplies. Here, turn south onto
Peach Road for a lovely ride going uphill and down, past an old

log cabin and between marshy lakes. Keep on
heading south and you'll soon see the
Chief Menominee Monument on
the left. Standing in a shady park,
the stately tribal leader is shown in
full regalia, his right palm upturned.
Chief Menominee once tried to oppose the governor's orders
to force his people out of the Twin Lakes region. The chief
and a band of 859 Potawatomi men, women, and children were
driven from their prairie homes in 1838 and force-marched
over 900 miles to Kansas. This sad trek west has been vari-
ously called the Trail of Death, the Trail of Tears, and the Trail
of Courage. Chief Menominee himself died along the way
from typhoid fever. This memorial ground was set aside in
1909. From time to time visitors lay prairie grass or flowers
below the figure, a tribute to the tribal leader's great spirit.

When you leave the monument, turn left and drive south
along Peach Road to West Thirteenth Road. Turn left (east)
and left again on South Olive Trail. The valleys between the
ridges south of Plymouth are filled with glacial lakes. The
marshy patches here and there, lush with cattails, suggest terrain typical of an earlier time. South Olive Trail bisects
another pair of lakes, Lawrence on the right, Myers on the
left, where water lilies float in dappled sunlight. Patches of
pale blue and orange flowers bloom beside the road. South
Olive Trail ends at SR 17, so follow this route into Plymouth.

SR 17 enters Plymouth on La Porte Street, which has several
restaurants. Drive north along the main thoroughfare,
Michigan Street, past colorful renovated shops and stores.
This street has evolved from the Old Michigan Road, when a
stagecoach line used to run through here between Logansport
and Michigan. Turn left off Michigan Street and go west on
Jefferson Street one block to find the courthouse square. The
Marshall County Courthouse is a Georgian revival structure

of white brick and stone. At the corner of Madison and Walnut Streets stands a stately brick house that was once the home of a state legislator and is now a funeral home. On the same block, at 317 West Monroe Street, you'll see a lovely renovated carriage house (vintage 1889) of painted gray brick.

For More Information

Jasper-Pulaski Fish & Wildlife Area (Medaryville): 219-843-4841

Tefft Savanna Nature Preserve (Department of Natural Resources; Indianapolis): 765-232-4200

Bass Lake State Beach (Knox): 219-772-3382

The Shore Club (Knox): 219-772-3363

Culver Marina: 219-842-3375

Culver Military Academy: 219-842-7000

Plymouth Chamber of Commerce: 219-936-2323

Marshall County Convention & Visitors' Bureau (Plymouth): 800-626-5353

4

Tracks Across
the Plains

Monon to Fort Ouiatenon

Getting there: From Indianapolis, take I-65 northwest to SR 18. Follow SR 18 east to SR 43 and head north to Reynolds. Continue north on U.S. 421 to Monon. From the Chicago area, take I-80/90 to I-65. Exit on SR 10 and drive east to U.S. 421, then south to Monon.

Highlights: sample small-town America; paddle down a scenic river, visit a historic battlefield, and observe bison and wolves in a supervised habitat; unwind near the site of an early French fort.

The fertile prairie around you, now productive farmland, once spread all the way from Indiana to the Mississippi River. Ahead along the horizon lies a fuzzy line of trees and the highway shrinks to infinity. Drive into Monon amid clustered houses and great old trees, the water tower rising above them. This is a family town where residents fly the nation's flag proudly, and everyone turns out for Little League games. Drive through the town park on the west side, and folks wave in greeting as you pass. Beside the creek, you may see a family picnicking in a grove of trees.

Follow SR 16 east from Monon and you're on your way to Buffalo. Great herds of bison once grazed these plains, their numbers held in check by packs of wolves. The road you drive cuts between squared-off fields of corn and beans, a patchwork of earthy colors. Indiana has become a major producer of corn, hogs, and soybeans; this area is known for popcorn, mint, garden vegetables, and fruit. Early farmers tilled their fields with teams of horses or sturdy oxen. Today's farmers ride in air-conditioned tractor cabs, listening to the stereo.

Turn right and go south on SR 39 toward Monticello along Lake Shafer, formed by the Norway Dam. You'll see tan, scruffy cattle grazing in the fields and possibly deer. Be alert for deer that suddenly leap farm fences onto the highway right into your path. Packs of wolves no longer keep deer populations in check; instead, hunters in season now cull the herds that inhabit the forests. Study the landscape and you could well see a cardinal, the Indiana state bird, flit from fence post to treetop.

The town of Monticello, at the junction of SR 39 and U.S. 24, has grown between two lakes, Shafer and Freeman, formed by the waters of the Tippecanoe River. In early times, the Potawatomi Indians called the Tippecanoe "place of the buffalo fish." In all, this scenic waterway flows about 220 miles to join the Wabash River. Wooded lots, cottages, and year-round lakeside homes can be found all around Monticello. SR 39 and U.S. 24 take you west into town, a trading center for the resort community. Notice the brick building housing the First National Bank. It really does look like Thomas Jefferson's home.

Head out U.S. 24 west past the Tree House Restaurant, convenient for sit-down snacks or a meal. Continue on U.S. 24 west, turn north on Sixth Street, and follow the signs to Indiana Beach, about five miles. This lakeside resort has amusement park rides, a boardwalk, shops, eating places, games, a sandy swimming beach, and more. After opening for weekends only in early May, it stays open daily from 11:00 A.M. to 11:00 P.M. from mid-May through Labor Day.

After the honky-tonk, cotton-candy fun at Indiana Beach, return to Monticello and drive south along the east side of Lake Freeman on U.S. 421/SR 39 for about eight miles. Cool your sunburn on a lovely canoe ride down the scenic, partly shady Tippecanoe River below the dam. At the sign for Hodges Float Trips, turn right on CR 600 north and take time for one of the river excursions. Paddling down this lovely, easy river (this stretch is Class I) for 12 miles takes about three to four hours and is well worth the time. Owners Robert and Judith Bartlett rent canoes by the day. They'll go over safety rules with you and hand out regulation jackets and cushions. You can put the canoe in at their riverside home.

Paddle downstream and the river resembles a tunnel, with overarching branches. You'll almost certainly see some kind of wildlife—foxes, beavers, hawks, deer, nesting eagles, or blue herons. Here and there, little islands or sandbars invite you to rest. Fishermen talk about the small-mouth bass, striped bass, river perch, channel cats (catfish), and walleyes here. When you finish the run, the Bartletts haul you and the canoe back upstream.

Return to U.S. 421 and drive south to SR 18. Turn west to find a wider, statelier Tippecanoe River flowing beneath the bridge at Springboro, where white dogwood trees bloom in the spring. The drive winds through a forested valley, and you travel west into Brookston. There you'll find Klein Brot Haus, a European-style bakery-cafe, on Main Street. Enter the 1903 brick building under the blue-striped awnings to enjoy the pots of cactus on tables with checkered cloths, as well as the home-cooked food.

Kathy Richards, who started it all in the late 1970s, began selling bread she baked at home. Grinding the wheat herself for better nutrition, she then sold a mixed-grain bread in a family-owned market. The first bread was terrible, she claims. "It tasted good but didn't slice well; it would just crumble." That didn't seem to matter, though. After some newspaper publicity, Kathy says, "people were standing in line" to buy it. "They even bought raw dough." Eventually, with help from others, Richards refined the recipes, gave up baking at home, and opened the Klein Brot Haus, serving a luncheon buffet with homemade soup and sandwiches made with these special breads. The cafe is also open evenings. For dessert, try the Linzer Torte, hand-rolled Danish, or thick blueberry pies. The Texas cinnamon rolls are legendary.

From Brookston's Main Street, drive south on SR 43. Pass the first turnoff to the village of Battle Ground, go under I-65, and, just beyond, turn onto Prophet's Rock Road toward Battle Ground. Go over a hill, through the woods, and you'll see Prophet's Rock on the left, about 30 feet high. An Indian known as the Prophet once stood on this bluff urging Shawnees to attack William Henry Harrison's troops. During the fight, the Prophet reportedly stayed at the rock, praying to the Great Spirit for success.

Drive on into Battle Ground on Prophet's Rock Road, into the village "downtown"—the cafe, laundromat, and grocery at the junction of several streets and the railroad. Across the way, you can usually find potter Scott Frankenberger in his workshop afternoons, but it's best to call ahead. An award winner at art shows and exhibitions throughout the Midwest, Frankenberger makes handsome, functional porcelain pieces. His work has been bought for private collections throughout the world. Prices range from $5 to $125, with the typical piece being $20 or $25.

Follow Main Street and the signs out of Battle Ground to Wolf Park. You'll turn onto Jefferson Street, which becomes a rocky country road with lavender flowers blooming in the spring. A sign marks the entrance to Wolf Park. Here ethologists, aided by volunteers, study the behavior of wolves and bison. Visitors can see the animals in the park daily (except on holidays) between 1:00 P.M. and 5:00 P.M. from May through November. The wolves might be walking around, feeding, napping, snapping playfully at one another—or observing human behavior through the chain-link fence. Docents at the park can answer your questions. On Saturdays and Sundays at 1:00 P.M., weather permitting, visitors may watch wolves and bison mingle with one another on the bison range, observing the ways wolves test their prey and learning how bison protect themselves and their calves. Wolf Park staff prevent the animals from injuring one another in these encounters. On Saturday nights year-round and on Friday nights in season, visitors may attend wolf howl nights to learn about wolf communication.

Return to Battle Ground and drive south (follow the signs) to the Tippecanoe Battlefield Museum. Operated by the Tippecanoe County Historical Association, the museum has two sections. Inside on the left, exhibits explain the history and background of the Battle of Tippecanoe, which erupted over a conflict between two cultures. Hostilities grew as treaties were made and broken and promises dishonored. Finally, Indiana territorial governor William Henry Harrison led troops north from Vincennes toward Prophetstown, the Shawnee village. The braves attacked the soldiers' encampment at around 4:00 A.M. on November 7, 1811. With the Shawnee leader Tecumseh away, his brother gave the order to attack. Almost 900 soldiers fought about 700 Indians for about three hours before the Indian forces withdrew. The battle was a turning point;

Tecumseh was never able to form an Indian confederacy after that. Harrison's victory opened up this region for settlement. At the other end of the museum, a gift shop displays period clothing, historic books and maps, and handcrafted items.

Across the parking lot, the Tippecanoe Battlefield Memorial marks the site of Harrison's encampment and the battle. Today, the grassy headland with stately old trees is quite peaceful, a national historic landmark.

West of the parking lot, visit the small but excellent Waba-shika Nature Center. Concrete steps descend a hill toward Burnett's Creek where a sign marks the start of the Wabash Heritage Trail. You can hike this nine-mile trail past woodland where birds twitter and squirrels scamper past Burnett's Creek, which flows into the Wabash River. The first segment of the trail crosses the old Davis Ferry Bridge, ending at Davis Ferry Park. The second section runs from Davis Ferry Park beside the Wabash to Riehle Plaza in downtown Lafayette.

Leave Battle Ground via Prophet's Rock Road, return to SR 43, and drive south toward Lafayette. Tecumseh Trail Park, a wooded picnic spot between the highway and the Wabash River, is on the route used by the Indians—including Chief Tecumseh—on journeys between villages.

Across from the park, a paved road ascends the hill by a series of switchbacks to the Indiana Veterans' Home. The early commandant's residence, which overlooks the river valley, has been made into a B&B serving formal breakfasts. This sloped and wooded hillside sprouts patches of wildflowers in spring, and the brittle, clinging leaves radiate gold and crimson in the fall. Continue south on SR 43 and you'll enter West Lafayette via North River Road.

Turn left and go east across the Harrison Bridge, named for the governor who led the forces at Battle Ground. To the right, downstream, you can see the levee where Lafayette's founder, William Digby, used to run a ferry service across to Brown Street. For a time, there was a wooden covered bridge here, built to facilitate travel between the towns.

On the east (right) side of the bridge, on Union Street, you'll find the Pub, a dark, cheerfully noisy restaurant and bar usually bustling with bankers, housewives, Purdue University professors, secretaries, and construction workers. Around old wooden tables, they wash down hot sandwiches or lavish salads with cold Cokes or beer.

Head east on one-way Union Street and drive to Ninth Street. Go right and head south to the intersection of Ninth and Main Streets. Here, on Main Street for two blocks east and west, you'll discover antique and gift shops to please any shopper—Main Street Mercantile, One Earth, Buck Creek Book Store, and the Antique Mall. U.S. travelers from either coast comment on the good buys they get here in Midwest shops. For a special weekday lunch, try Sarge Oak on Main, at 721 Main Street, a steak house with a renovated interior, good service, and a chef with imagination. The Lafayette Brewing Company, 622 Main Street, serves tasty lunches and evening meals.

From the corner of Ninth and South Streets, you can see a striking hilltop building done in Gothic revival style. The Moses Fowler Chase Mansion, built by an early real estate speculator, was once a family residence. For a time, it boasted a formal Italian garden to the south, complete with reflecting pool and teahouse. Now, the Tippecanoe County Historical Association has offices and a museum here.

On Columbia Street, one block north and parallel to South Street, drive west through Lafayette's city center. Between May and October, the farmer's market on Fifth Street (between Main and Columbia) sells fresh vegetables, fruits, homemade breads, preserves, and flowers in the morning, three days a week. The vendors back up vehicles to the sidewalk and display their colorful produce on card tables.

Across from the market stands the Knickerbocker, the oldest saloon in Indiana still operating. Known for its wide selection of beer, the renovated lounge draws standing-room-only crowds on weekends whenever guest bands play live jazz.

Continue west on Columbia Street past the Tippecanoe County Courthouse, whose dome rises 212 feet above the ground. The Goddess of Liberty stands there above female figures symbolizing the four seasons in niches below. At the corner of Third and Columbia Streets, the Maize serves American cuisine.

Continue west on Columbia Street for a drive over Lafayette's newest bridge, completed in 1992. You'll pass the old Purdue Block buildings and the levee on the right. When you reach the intersection at SR 43, take SR 26 west up State Street hill into West Lafayette's downtown. Known simply as the Village, this group of shops, restaurants, and pubs is a good place to stretch your legs, explore for bargains, pick up some souvenirs, and stop in at a restaurant or pub for lunch or an afternoon break and rub elbows with students from Purdue University.

Explore the three-block area along State Street between Grant and Chauncey Streets, where Purdue students from all over the world, including young Muslim women covered with fabric from their heads down to their Reeboks, shop for necessities. Creative types put together wardrobes of ethnic and vintage clothing for little cash at Amused Clothing. At Vienna Espresso Bar, grad students and salespeople sip exotic coffees. The South Street Grill at South and Chauncey serves delicious, freshly made dishes.

Across State Street, at the far end of Chauncey Mall, the Parthenon serves good Greek food. Von's Book Shop on State Street, crammed with paperbacks on every subject, was formerly located in a big old house one block south. When John Von Erdmannsdorff started the bookstore in his home, customers had to knock on the locked door and hope someone would come to let them in!

At the corner of Pierce and State Streets, Harry's Chocolate Shop (run by the people who operate the Pub) is a student pub with good food, done in animal-house chic. Peek in at the scarred wooden tables and graffiti-brightened walls, and if you're hungry, get a cheeseburger, the best in town. Harry's Chocolate Shop opened in 1919 during Prohibition and really did sell sodas and ice cream concoctions. Some insist the early owners sold home-brewed beer as well, flaunting the law at the time.

West on State Street is Purdue University's main campus. Since it began as a land-grant college in 1874, the university has graduated more than 300,000 alumni. Computer printouts now list graduates living and working around the world; there's even a linguist on remote Tagula Island in Papua New Guinea. For more information about the university, stop at the visitors' center at 504 Northwestern Avenue.

When you've finished wandering around West Lafayette, drive south of State Street one block to Wood Street, and follow it east downhill. Turn right onto South River Road and cruise along the bottomland of the Wabash River about four miles toward Fort Ouiatenon. You'll see a log replica of a blockhouse at Fort Ouiatenon County Park that is set among trees and grass beside the Wabash.

Established in 1717, Fort Ouiatenon was the first fortified European settlement in what is now Indiana and functioned as a trading post while trying to prevent British expansion. Around the early fort and across the river were many Wea Indian villages, constituting one of the largest Native American settlements in the Midwest. After the blockhouse was built, archaeologists dug to discover the actual site of the

French fort about a mile downriver. The site is now in the *National Register of Historic Places.*

By the early nineteenth century, the fort lay in ruins, no longer considered useful. Fortunately for us today, the area teems with life during the Feast of the Hunter's Moon, an annual festival celebrating the return of the voyageurs from their arduous travels. Traditional crafts, costumes, tomahawk contests, foods, music, and games simulate activities that people enjoyed in an earlier time.

For More Information

Monticello Chamber of Commerce: 219-583-7220

Indiana Beach (Monticello): 219-583-4141

Klein Brot Haus and Bakery, Inc. (Brookston): 765-563-3788

Greater Lafayette Convention and Visitors' Bureau (Lafayette): 765-447-9999 or 800-872-6648

Scott Frankenberger (Battle Ground): 765-567-2678

Wolf Park (Battle Ground): 765-567-2265

Tippecanoe Battlefield Museum (Battle Ground): 765-567-2147

Tippecanoe County Historical Association (Lafayette): 765-476-8411

Tippecanoe County Park and Recreation Department (West Lafayette): 765-463-2306

Purdue University Visitors' Center (West Lafayette): 765-494-4636

5

Wildflowers & Lake Country

Pokagon State Park to Gene Stratton Porter House

Getting there: From Indianapolis, take I-69 north to the exit for Pokagon State Park and follow the signs. From Chicago, take I-80/90 east across Indiana to the Angola/Pokagon exit. Follow the signs south and west to Pokagon State Park.

Highlights: have family fun in winter, or stroll past wildflower gardens in spring and summer; take a scenic flight over mirror lakes; visit an authentic gristmill in operation.

Northeastern Indiana has long been known for glacial lakes, forests, streams, and patches of wildflowers. You can come by interstate, but once you arrive, follow the country roads to find nature preserves, hiking trails, boat rentals, small villages, antique shops, family resorts, and scenic waterways. At one airport, a pilot will take you in a small plane to view all this scenery from 5,000 feet.

Start this drive at 1,203-acre Pokagon State Park on the eastern shore of Lake James, the fourth largest lake in Indiana. Pokagon may well be Indiana's most popular year-round park, for people come in winter to go sledding down the hills, ski across the hillsides, and skate on the frozen lake. Tobogganers shriek with delight when they discover the 1,780-foot-long toboggan slide and go swooping down the incline. The diehards then climb back up to do it all again.

Within the park, the newly refurbished Potawatomi Inn (vintage 1927) overlooks the lake and has facilities for boating, fishing, and waterskiing. Named for the Indian tribe that once inhabited this region, the 81-room resort offers real value for families, with its no-alcohol policy, informal dining room, library, indoor swimming pool, and sauna. When families come here for reunions, the youngsters usually keep busy. The friendly staff makes everyone comfortable, from babies to great-grannies.

The state park itself was named for the Potawatomi chief, Leopold Pokagon, and his son, Simon. At one time the elder Pokagon sold roughly a million acres of land to the U.S. government—for three cents an acre. He then retired at a lake in Michigan to live out his days. The younger Pokagon, educated at Notre Dame prep school and Oberlin College, was widely known on the lecture circuit for his expertise on Native American culture and special issues.

From Pokagon State Park, take SR 727 to SR 127 south to reach Angola, the Steuben County seat. A former college student who lived in Fort Wayne confided, "On weekends, we used to pile in a car and drive to Angola—just to go around the traffic circle." In the center of this well-known circle is a monument to Civil War veterans. Atop the 85-foot monument stands a statue of Columbia, a sylphlike female figure holding a flag. Around the circle are shops, a movie theater, and cafes—in a very walkable town center. At lunchtime, try Cafe

Steuben County

on the Mound. Also, visit the Steuben County Tourism Bureau at 207 South Wayne Street to learn more about the area's antique shops, historic B&Bs, and golf courses.

Named for a town in New York State, Angola grew at the place where the road from Fort Wayne to Michigan crossed the old Maumee Trail. Early shopkeepers traded with Indians living nearby, and the town's first settlers often came to town on horseback or in wagons drawn by oxen. The names of the town's settlers—Gale, Martha, Gilmore, and Elizabeth—are on the street signs around the central square.

From the circle, take U.S. 20 directly west. This route, Maumee Street, leads to the Hartman House (901 West Maumee), a bed-and-breakfast inn with a fine restaurant and wine bar. Chef Linda, who has studied at Le Cordon Bleu, prepares entrees like baked pork loin with apricot sauce and four-layer chocolate torte. The route continues west past the Tri-State University campus on the left. On the 400-acre grounds you'll find a museum housing memorabilia of Gen. Lewis B. Hershey, a Tri-State alumnus. Hershey directed the U.S. Selective Service between 1941 and 1970. Some veterans of World War II remember his signature on their draft cards. U.S. 20 west also passes the Steuben County Museum, housed in a vintage family home. At 200 west turn north, go three-fourths of a mile, and turn at the sign for the Buck Lake Ranch, a mini-Nashville where Johnny Cash, Patsy Cline, and Elvis Presley all performed. Return to U.S. 20 west.

As you drive along, the traffic eventually thins and you pass a tranquil pond covered with lily pads on the right. Beyond I-69 the road stretches over rolling hills, skirts small farms, and edges a mirror lake. At Steuben County Municipal Airport, five miles west of Angola on the right, Tri-State Airways offers scenic flights daily the year 'round but is closed on Christmas Day. If you hang around, you can watch flight students practice touch-and-go's (takeoffs and landings). Take a scenic flight, and you'll buckle up in a high-wing plane, soon to be wafting over Crooked Lake. Ask the pilot to show you Mt. Tamarack, a cone-shaped hill that's the highest ground around. Through the plane window, you can make out water-skiers on Lake James, a strip of beach downhill from the Potawatomi Inn, Snow Lake, Lake George, and Feather Valley Road. Eventually, the town of Angola comes around, looking like a doll village set among broccoli stalks. The cost of a scenic flight runs about $12 to $15 per person for a 20-minute ride. Tri-State Airways suggests you call at least half an hour ahead to make arrangements for one, two, or three people. With more notice, they'll round up a larger plane for four or more.

After a stop at the airport, continue west on U.S. 20, curving past Otter Lake to SR 327, and turn north. You'll drive past fields, marshes, and forests along the boundary of Steuben County. Known for its 101 lakes, the county also has wildflowers that change with each season. The daylilies look festive in front of neatly tended homes.

The town of Orland, settled around 1835, could well be the oldest community in the county. When there's no traffic at all, you can stand at the intersection (SRs 327 and 120), look about in four directions, and see the entire town!

Take SR 120 west of Orland, and you'll soon enter Lagrange County. Here more than 40 percent of the population is Old Order Amish, living on farms in the traditional way. One mile west of the county line, turn right on CR 1100 east, a paved road through hilly, forested land and cornfields. Keep going when the road becomes gravel, to a pond where wild ducks often swim, and turn sharply left onto a road through dense woodland. You'll eventually see a sign for CR 1060 east and it will segue into CR 1050 east, to run north along the pond at Greenfield Mills.

In this village, in a rickety brick-and-siding structure, the Rinkel family carries on an old tradition that goes back four generations—grinding grain into flour. When Howard Rinkel's grandfather bought the run-down mill in 1904, he built it into a thriving business. Poke around inside the building today, and you'll chuckle at shelves stacked with five-pound bags of "New Rinkel" flour. The family all pitches in to turn out their certified organic white and whole-wheat flour.

Greenfield Mills, Inc., stands at the site of an old mill that was built around 1846. Helen Rinkel, a young Iowa girl, met her husband, Howard, at church when he was a student. He convinced her to marry him and brought her back to Greenfield Mills. "I had to learn to cook all over again," she recalls. The wheat flour in Indiana came from soft wheat, she explains, and she'd been baking with hard wheat flour. Now, the Rinkels sell bread flour that's a blend of both.

Head south from Greenfield Mills via CR 1060 east and CR 1100 east back to SR 120, and go west to Brighton. This little burg was the site of a short-lived commune during the mid-nineteenth century. Established by a religious group turning away from "evil" civilization, the group quickly fell apart.

From Brighton, turn south onto SR 3 and drive to Mongo. This country road passes a lovely little church reminiscent of New England. The village of Mongo, well off the usual Indiana tourist routes, consists of a few stores that flank the main drag and assorted homes and cottages along a grid of shady lanes. Mongo took root at the site of an early Indian village after fur traders from Fort Wayne built a trading post. The Indian name comes from a much longer word meaning "big squaw."

Outdoor people love adventures on the Pigeon River, and Mongo has become their headquarters. Fishermen and women find bluegill, bass, pike, and trout in the river and nearby lakes. The 11,500-acre Pigeon River Fish and Wildlife Area extends from Mongo along the river to the east and west. In season, hunters stalk deer, doves, squirrels, waterfowl, turkeys, and other game. Because there is so little development along the riverbanks, the area is rich in wildlife. Ponds covered with water lilies entice various kinds of waterfowl. Bird-watchers, campers, and hikers find everything here from frogs to pheasants.

Head west of Mongo on CR 300 north over a paved road that passes Trading Post Outfitters. This company organizes canoe trips on the scenic Pigeon River and also runs a campground. There are various put-in spots along the way, so you can have anything from an hour-and-a-half paddle to an all-day run. The shallow river flows gently but twists a lot, and paddlers pass under several bridges.

CR 300 north winds toward the village of Ontario, meandering through wild country resembling the landscape of an earlier time. Early travelers through this territory often mentioned the region's copious water supply, its fertile soil, and the beautiful growth of forest. Drive here early in the morning and a fine mist rises from foliage made lush and green from recent rains. Pines, oaks, and other hardwoods, along with patches of wildflowers, thrive in the rich prairie soil.

From Ontario, once a thriving industrial town, continue west on CR 225 until you reach SR 9. Turn left and head south to Lagrange, a small town with downtown stores around the red-brick Renaissance revival courthouse that has been the county seat since 1844. The town has shade trees and old, brick streets, yet it bustles with activity as people come from miles around to trade. A woman in black bonnet and plain dress pulls her two small boys across the grassy lawn. A black buggy and horse, hitched to a railing, await them on the far side.

Drive south on SR 9 and pass through Valentine to Wolcottville. Note that shop owners have organized a tiny mall here. Continue on through Rome. One mile south of the town, turn east at the sign for Gene Stratton Porter State Historical Site on the shore of Sylvan Lake. At the turn of the century, vacationers came to Sylvan Lake to stay in small hotels or cottages, and there was a dance hall and an ice cream parlor on an island in the lake. At the time, a bridge connected the dance hall to the railroad station, and visitors who preferred not to promenade along the bridge boarded a lake steamer used as a passenger ferry to the island.

As you turn in toward the historic site, you'll discover a sheltered picnic area near the parking lot and a rusty pump that may (or may not) bring up water from a well. Hike down a gravel path toward Sylvan Lake and you'll pass the grave of author, naturalist, and photographer Geneva "Gene" Stratton Porter, who was born in 1863 and died in Los Angeles during the 1920s. Nearby, various clubs have planted trees in her memory.

Walk toward the gardens and Porter's lakeside home, and you'll see black-eyed Susans, coralbells, spirea, and impatiens that bloom here and there in the forest. If you have any questions about the plants, ask the on-site naturalist. The log "cabin" where Porter lived is, in fact, a two-story home of white cedar and native stone. The author referred to it as the "cabin in Wildflower Woods." Porter lived and worked at this home from 1914 to 1919, using details of the setting in bestselling books, but she is best known for the novel *A Girl of the Limberlost*, written at another log home near Geneva, Indiana. Publishers at one time claimed the author had 50 million readers in the United States alone. During the last 17 years of her life, Porter's books sold at the rate of 1,700 copies a day. Wide concrete steps lead to the front porch of Porter's home on Sylvan Lake. Urns of flowers sit atop the wall. From the front walk leading to the boat dock, take a lakeshore path left to find the Morning Face bench. In the woodland quiet beside the lake, just as Gene Stratton Porter did, you can hear water lapping against the shore and frogs croaking somewhere in the shadows and see ducks paddling about the lake, dipping their heads down to feed in the water.

For More Information

All numbers are within area code 219.

Steuben County Tourism Bureau (Angola): 665-5386, 800-LAKE-101, or 800-581-0908

Pokagon State Park (Angola): 833-2012

Potawatomi Inn (Angola): 833-1077

The Hartman House (Angola): 665-9080 or 800-909-9080

Tri-State Airways (Angola): 665-3212

Trading Post Outfitters (Mongo): 367-2493

Gene Stratton Porter State Historical Site: 854-3790

6

Literary History
& the Heartland

Crawfordsville to Rockville

Getting there: From Indianapolis, take I-74 west to SR 231. Exit south to Crawfordsville, where the tour begins. From Chicago, take I-80/90 to I-65 and drive southeast to Lebanon. Take SR 32 west to Crawfordsville.

Highlights: canoeing on a scenic creek, strolling through a historic district, and hiking rugged park trails; covered bridges, the Maple Fair, and Ernie Pyle's boyhood home.

Begin the drive with a visit to the Linden Railroad Museum, housed in a vintage depot once used by the Monon Railroad. Then follow SR 231 south to Crawfordsville. In the Sugar Creek Valley today you won't see many signs of the Indians who used to hunt here, the Kickapoo, Miami, Shawnee, Potawatomi, and other tribes, who paddled scenic Sugar Creek in birch-bark canoes. What better way to explore the creek with its covered bridges than by paddling a canoe downstream?

Clements Canoes, Inc., offers liveried canoe trips of several lengths along this waterway. Most of the canoe routes lead through rock canyons, under covered bridges, and past historic landmarks. Islands and sandbars make enticing spots to stop and picnic along the way. Whippoorwills call, and waterfalls, often used as cool showers in hot, sticky weather, cascade down rough rock canyon walls. When the water is high, paddling through the channel west of Crawfordsville gives you a white-water trip (Class II, four to six hours). As the water surges downstream, rushing through narrows and swirling around rocks, it winds for 15 miles to Deer's Mill Covered Bridge. Clements Canoes offers different routes for shorter or longer time periods.

Crawfordsville nestles in a valley formed by Sugar Creek. Enter the town via SR 231 from either direction and you're on Washington Street, Crawfordsville's main thoroughfare; here collectors will enjoy the large Cabbages and Kings antiques mall. Sometimes called the Athens of Indiana, the town has a historic reputation for culture and learning. A surprising number of writers, artists, statesmen, and other notables spent their formative years in this town of a few thousand people.

All of Crawfordsville's historic buildings have been organized into a walking tour. Stop at the visitors' center to get a map showing their locations. Before that, you may want to view the well-known Lane Place. At the sign for Visitor Information, turn east onto Pike Street and go two blocks to see the impressive, two-story Lane Place, just beyond the intersection of Water and Pike Streets. This white-brick building with Corinthian columns stands on a breezy, shaded hill where roses bloom in season. Built in Greek Revival style, Lane Place was once the residence of Henry S. Lane, Indiana's first Republican governor, an associate of Abraham Lincoln. A brick walkway leads to the front portico of the building, now in the *National Register of Historic Places*. Deeded to the

Montgomery County Historical Society in 1931, Lane Place stays open Tuesday through Sunday, April through October.

Another red-brick walk on the grounds leads to a pre–Civil War cabin that became a Crawfordsville "station" on the Underground Railroad. Brought here from Grant and North Streets, this 15-by-20-foot cabin was the home of John Allen Speed and his wife, Margaret. Active in the antislavery movement, Speed helped fugitives hide in the loft before their secret journey to the next station.

During the late nineteenth century and into the twentieth, Indiana was known for its authors. Edward Eggleston's *The Hoosier Schoolmaster*, Lew Wallace's *Ben Hur*, Maurice Thompson's *Alice of Old Vincennes*, Gene Stratton Porter's *Freckles*, Booth Tarkington's *Penrod*, and Theodore Dreiser's *An American Tragedy* were widely read during that period. At the time, there seemed to be no explanation for Indiana's literary output, and one author suggested, "Maybe it's something in the drinking water."

A block farther east on Pike Street, behind a square brick wall, there's a three-story brick building, built by Gen. Lew Wallace, which is now the Ben Hur Museum. To the west of the building a bronze statue of Governor Wallace stands in the place where he used to sit. Shaded by a giant beech tree, Wallace sat outside in a rocking chair to write portions of the popular novel, *Ben Hur: A Tale of the Christ*. Wallace, from a prominent Hoosier family, lived in Crawfordsville between 1853 and 1905. Known best for *Ben Hur*, published in 1880, Wallace used royalties from this bestselling novel to build his Crawfordsville home. On the lower floor, you'll see a relic French Victoria carriage made for Wallace in Paris in 1873. Nearby stands Wallace's old leather-covered Morris chair. Wallace used the large main room, lined with bookshelves, as a study.

JoAnne Sprague, native Hoosier and lifelong Indiana resident, has been curator of the museum since 1988. "He's an incredible man," she says in summary. "Minister to Turkey, soldier, state senator, art collector, governor (of the New Mexico Territory). He led a fascinating life."

Examine the walls of Wallace's study, decorated with memorabilia. An ornamental rug was a gift from the sultan of Persia. Movie stills depict scenes from the award-winning film *Ben Hur*, based on his most famous novel. The Wallace family silver service rests on a shelf. In one photo, author Wallace rocks in a chair beneath the legendary beech tree, which later came down. Other shelves hold sheet music for a favorite song, "Annie Laurie." An article about Wallace appeared in the 1898 *Ladies' Home Journal*.

One section of the wall displays volumes of Wallace's works: *The Fair God*, set in Mexico; *The Prince of India*; and of course, *Ben Hur*, set in Rome during the early years of Christianity; and many others. After Wallace died, he was buried in Crawfordsville's Oak Grove Cemetery.

Restaurants change, so check with the locals. The former Cafe 127 at 127 Green Street, for example, has become Joe's Bar and Grill. Or try Doodles, known for soups and salads; at 127 South Green Street, it's an easy walk from Lane Place or the Ben Hur Museum.

Return to 225 North Washington Street for a look at the Old Jail Museum, built in 1882. The building has a unique rotary cell block, still in operation (without the prisoners), and interesting exhibits.

From the Old Jail Museum, drive south on Washington Street to SR 47, which veers to the right, and head west out of town into rolling countryside. The road meanders through farmland where a red-winged blackbird may take flight above a corn-field. Here and there, the lawns of homes are brightened by red or pink peonies, the Indiana state flower.

Via a detour on old U.S. 32, you can reach a small bed and breakfast that boasts a spot in the *National Register of Historic Places*. Experience history as a guest in the two-story brick Yount's Mill Inn, which was built in 1851 by an early settler and has four guest rooms, each uniquely decorated. The Rose Room has a four-poster bed and a dressing alcove. The Green Room, with an antique double bed, has a view of an old wooden mill that is also in the *National Register.* The Green Room, the Primitive Room, and the Lace Room all have creek views. The new owners have been remodeling the historic woolen mill behind the inn to turn it into a conference center.

Return to SR 47 via the same route and continue west. Just after you cross Indian Creek, turn right on SR 234 and drive north toward Shades State Park. The road skims the tops of low hills. At the sign for Clements Canoes, go straight to the entrance of the park.

A hiker's delight, Shades State Park contains more than eight miles of trails, through Shawnee Canyon, past Lover's Leap overlooking Sugar Creek, and along the Devil's Punch Bowl. The heavily forested 3,084-acre reserve was the site of a health resort during the nineteenth century. Now Shades State Park also contains a 3,000-foot-long grassy landing strip and a parking area for small planes. Called simply "the Shades" by local people, Shades State Park was once known as the Shades of Death; several stories are told to explain this name. One claims that deep shadows in this black forest suggest death. Another says that warlike Indians living in this woodland killed an early settler here. Yet another claims a young wife killed her abusive husband here with a woodsman's ax.

After exploring the park, return to SR 234 and drive north. In season, golden wildflowers bloom along the road. On the left, you'll see an entrance to Pine Hills Nature Preserve. Receding glaciers left four ridges that form the backbones of Pine Hills.

SR 234 crosses Sugar Creek over a new bridge. As you cross, you can see the red Deer's Mill Covered Bridge to the left. To the right and below, water tumbles over a rocky creek bed. Early settlers noticed the sandstone cliffs, deep ravines, and dense forests along Sugar Creek and chose to clear flatter land nearby for farming. Thus, stands of virgin timber along Sugar Creek have been preserved and protected in state parks and preserves.

Continue along SR 234, which winds beneath a canopy of greenery, crosses streams that bubble through the forest into Sugar Creek, stretches out over the crests of hills, and reaches down into valleys. Someone built a log cabin here, set in a clearing. And beyond all this, on higher, flatter ground, you'll see more farmland. At the intersection of SR 234 and U.S. 41, turn south toward Turkey Run State Park to drive straight through the heart of the country. After crossing Sugar Creek, turn left again at SR 47 and follow signs to the park entrance.

Open all year, scenic Turkey Run State Park has one of the largest stands of virgin timber left in Indiana. Campers, hikers, horseback riders, bicyclists, and picnickers can do their thing in a setting of wooded ravines, sandstone cliffs, and covered bridges over Sugar Creek. Most of Turkey Run's cliffs are Mansfield sandstone, a sedimentary rock formed from sand. Wind, water, and scouring debris from glacial action shaped the sandstone into the interesting forms you see today. For centuries, Miami Indians hunted this land and fished these streams. Explore the park today, and you can use marked trails.

Cross the bridge over Sugar Creek to Rocky Hollow Falls Canyon Nature Preserve. Here, waterfalls splash onto rocky streambeds, and the water flows through ancient forests with evergreens, black walnut trees, sycamores, and oaks. Rugged Trail 2 runs along the base of sandstone cliffs, and challenging Trail 3 follows rough terrain between Rocky Hollow and Bear Hollow.

From the Turkey Run State Park entrance, turn left on SR 47 and then north on CR 300 east. The paved road crosses the

Narrows Covered Bridge, picturesque in this wooded setting of steep cliffs. In summer, the foliage turns myriad shades of green. In winter, a freezing rain may coat the bare branches with sparkling ice. Across the creek from the Narrows Covered Bridge, follow the road uphill to the Simon Lusk Homestead. This two-story structure of hand-fired brick was home to a miller who ran a gristmill on the creek for 21 years.

After the Lusk home, drive south across the Narrows Covered Bridge to return to SR 47. Turn right and go west to U.S. 41. At the highway, turn left and drive south toward the town of Rockville. Along U.S. 41 look for signs marking farms where Parke County farm people make traditional maple syrup. While everything they use is spotless and modern, they can tell you how the pioneers made syrup with wooden equipment.

During the 1800s, Hoosiers built many boxlike wooden bridges so horses wouldn't become frightened crossing the streams. Rural Parke County had the forethought to preserve 32 of these historic covered bridges. Now the autumn foliage season draws thousands of visitors and photographers. Despite heavy weekend traffic, autumn is a beautiful time to visit.

Rockville is the county seat in the covered-bridge capital of the world. Every October during the Covered Bridge Festival, motorists study color-coded maps before driving five routes looping in and out of Rockville. On any route you can see several covered bridges. Some bridges are no longer safe for traffic; others are still in use. At the Covered Bridge Festival, you can also watch arts and crafts demonstrations, shop at booths for local foods such as corn-on-the-cob, pork chops, and funnel cake, and hear musicians playing. For smaller crowds, go in late April or early May when flowering trees are in bloom. In late winter, Parke County holds a Maple Fair featuring tours to sugar camps. You can watch maple trees being tapped and sweet sap simmering before sampling the warm syrup on buttery pancakes. Displays of early equipment at the fair show how sap was collected in the past.

Open year-round, Billie Creek Village, located one and a third miles east of Rockville, consists of 30 pioneer buildings arranged beside a creek—with three covered bridges—on a 75-acre site. If you drive the Black route (on the Covered Bridge Festival map), you'll come to the village on your way back to Rockville. In Billie Creek Village you can watch blacksmiths at work, women at their looms, printers, and craftspeople showing you the everyday skills used by pioneers. You'll also see a general store, an old schoolhouse, a doctor's office, and much more. If you tire of walking, ride on the horse-drawn wagon.

Bridgeton, with painted homes and bright boxes of flowers, is another favorite village on the route. The old mill at Mansfield, reflected in a pond above the waterfall, graces many scenic postcards and calendars.

Complete this tour with a visit to the Ernie Pyle State Memorial at Dana. Drive west from Rockville via SR 36. Halfway to Dana, there's a rest park with an old covered bridge and a memorial in Pyle's honor. Enter Vermillion County and turn north on SR 71.

Born in 1900, Ernie Pyle lived in the white farmhouse you'll see coming north via SR 71 along Dana's main street. Moved here from another location, the house has become a museum featuring collections of the newspaper columns Pyle wrote, based on his worldwide travels and published in *Brave Men* and other books.

Pyle won a 1944 Pulitzer Prize for World War II reporting. He ended a book about soldiers in the European theater with these thoughts:

> That is our war, and we will carry it with us. I guess it doesn't make any difference, once a man has gone. Medals and speeches and victories are nothing to them any more.

They died and others lived and nobody knows why it is so.
They died, and thereby the rest of us can go on and on.*

Ernie Pyle never made it home. He was killed by a sniper's
fire on Ie Shima in 1945.

For More Information

All numbers are within area code 765.

Montgomery County Convention and Visitors' Bureau
(Crawfordsville): 362-5200 or 800-866-3973

Linden Railroad Museum: 339-7245

Clements Canoes, Inc. (Crawfordsville): 362-2781 or 362-9864

Henry S. Lane Mansion (Crawfordsville): 362-3416

Ben Hur Museum (Crawfordsville): 362-5769

Doodles (Crawfordsville): 361-9099

Old Jail Museum (Crawfordsville): 362-5222

The Marc Antiques (Crawfordsville): 362-1707

Yount's Mill Inn (West Crawfordsville): 362-5864

Shades State Park (Waveland): 435-2810

Turkey Run State Park (Marshall): 597-2635

Parke County Convention and Visitors' Bureau (Rockville):
569-5226

* From *Here Is Your War*, 1943, Henry Holt and Company, New York.

7

Exploring the Whitewater River Valley

Fountain City to Batesville

Getting there: From Chicago, take I-80/90 to I-65 to Indianapolis, then take I-70 east. North of Richmond, take SR 27 to Fountain City. From Columbus, Ohio, take I-70 west. After crossing the Indiana state line, exit on SR 27 north to Fountain City.

Highlights: visit a station on the Underground Railroad and a drive-through arboretum; shop for antiques, picnic beside an old canal, and ride on a vintage steam train.

Northeast of Fountain City is the highest elevation in Indiana, 1,257 feet. The headwaters of several rivers, including the Wabash, Whitewater, Miami, and White, flow from this high ground. In the village itself, a cluster of stores and houses are divided by U.S. 27; it's hard to believe that a modest house here was once a stopover for thousands of former slaves.

Start your journey through this fascinating region by visiting the Levi Coffin house, a state historic site in Fountain

57

City. The restored brick home, at the corner of U.S. 27 and Mill Street, was the first Hoosier building to make the *National Register of Historic Places.* Make an appointment and you can tour the inside.

Abolitionist Levi Coffin and his wife were among many Quakers who came to this region from the East. During the period when owning slaves was legal in states farther south, many people became wealthy from slave labor or by trading goods made by slaves. In 1831, Fountain City merchant Levi Coffin began limiting his sales to goods made by free workers. After the Civil War began, Coffin raised funds to help recently freed slaves who sought new lives in the industrial North. Over a 20-year period the Coffins helped more than 2,000 people.

In a cemetery near the Coffin house you'll find the grave of William Bush, a former slave aided by the Coffins. The greatgranddaughter of the man placed the marker on his grave in 1983.

After visiting the Levi Coffin home, drive south toward Richmond on U.S. 27. Just before the road widens, there's a turnoff for Arba Pike, a road following the early Quaker Trace. The Quaker settlers here built the rough road in an effort to improve trade with Fort Wayne. Continue south to Richmond, and U.S. 27 becomes Chester Boulevard.

In the early 1800s, when the first settlers realized the potential of the Whitewater River, they began building cabins in this area. At the time, only lands east of the Greenville Treaty line were open for settlement; lands to the west still belonged to the Indians. Goods sold in Richmond's first store came in on pack horses. Later, more goods from Cincinnati came in on horse-drawn wagons, traveling over nearly impassable roads.

Drive east of downtown, via U.S. 27 and South A Street to U.S. 40 east, to the Hayes Regional Arboretum along the route of the

Old National Road. This route has crossed Indiana since the 1830s, from Richmond through Centerville, Indianapolis, and Brazil to Terre Haute. At Elks Road, turn left at the sign for Hayes Regional Arboretum. The main gate is a half mile north. Privately owned but open to the public, the reserve has woody plants native to eastern Indiana, and you can either walk or drive through it.

First, stop at the nature center for the exhibits. Ask for a map of the route and a folder describing the trees. The three-and-a-half-mile self-drive tour runs through a dense forest. Clustered branches in leafy layers descend from the upper reaches to the forest floor. Here and there, signs identify white ash, hackberry, sugar maple, butternut, and hickory trees. Drive slowly to brake for a stray chipmunk or a Saturday morning jogger. The arboretum is also great to walk through, with trails that lead to a fern garden or to a spring house.

After the drive, exit onto Hayes Arboretum Road, turn right, and head west over the Old National Road. Beyond the golf course is Glenn Miller Park. Turn right inside the gates, and there's parking for the Richmond Rose Garden. These plantings were inspired by Richmond's Hill Roses Industry, the largest grower of roses under glass in the world. After adopting the name "Rose City" in the early 1970s, Richmond needed a public rose garden and therefore developed this one, containing about 1,600 rosebushes and other plantings. At peak times (June and September), many of the rosebushes are blooming amid greenery and brick walkways. Stroll past a white gazebo while water splashes from fountains, and listen to the hum of highway traffic along the road.

Return to U.S. 40 and drive east to the Promenade, a development two blocks wide along Main Street between Tenth and Fifth Streets. Stroll beneath shady "saucers" amid flowering plants and shrubs, and pass a splashing fountain. The Richmond Civic Theater now makes its home in the Murray Theater (1003 East Main Street), formerly an opera house.

Richmond residents have preserved many of the city's older homes—including those of the early elite—in the Starr Historic District between North A, North E, North Ninth, and North Sixteenth Streets. The Italianate mansion at 126 North Tenth Street was the residence of the Scott family for 119 years.

Drive south of the Promenade to the Olde Richmond Inn, at the corner of South Fifth and South B Streets. This charming neighborhood has become a historic district, in which you might see petunias cascading from the window boxes of a saltbox cottage, vintage 1854. The newer east-side addition of the Olde Richmond Inn disguises its charms. Within the main brick building, built in 1892, admire the original woodwork and chandeliers. Formerly a residence, the restaurant offers al fresco dining on the west terrace, beside the carriage house. Come for lunch or dinner; the menu lists salad plates, sandwich platters, steaks, and pastas. For a grand finale, try the black raspberry cobbler or a turtle sundae.

Return to U.S. 40 and head west (via North A, West Main, and Southwest First Streets). You'll pass Earlham College on the left, which was founded by Quakers. Continue on past a lovely park. This route follows the Old National Road for eight miles to Centerville.

Go to Jag's Cafe, 129 East Main Street in Centerville, for trendy food in a nostalgic setting (closed Mondays). Entering the old brick building that houses the restaurant, you'll be surprised to see the fronts of classic automobiles apparently coming through the walls. Sepia photos, antique signs, and even a mounted moosehead decorate exposed brick walls while ceiling fans whir above antique tables. A distinctive brick arch divides the dining area from the bar. The massive wooden back bar has ornate carved columns brought to Centerville from Chicago in 1893. Jag's features a lengthy menu of appetizers, soups, salads, snacks, sandwiches, steaks, and specialties. You could make a meal of the appetizers—like guacamole dip and miniburgers—or a dessert of the raspberry brie.

Known for its antiques mall, Centerville draws weekend crowds. The antiques are actually sold from quaint, older buildings along Morton and Main Streets. Dealer Verlon Webb started the Centerville mall with a small shop his father had. An auctioneer, he traveled the region buying antiques to sell for a profit. Entrepreneur Webb also helped decorate Jag's Cafe.

Quite a scene during the early nineteenth century, Centerville became crowded with row houses and covered alleys as traffic increased on the Old National Road. The coming of the railroad meant that Richmond ascended as Centerville declined. Even so, you'll still see more weekend shoppers in Centerville than at Richmond's Promenade.

Travel west on Main Street out of Centerville. On the north side, at 214 East Main Street, the Mansion House was once an inn where stagecoach passengers could spend the night. At West Main Street and Willow Grove, the terraced residence was once the home of Oliver Morton, an Indiana governor. Continue west on U.S. 40, following the signs to Dougherty's Orchard for crisp apples in autumn. In Pershing (also called East Germantown), look for a tiny shop with homemade quilts.

Where U.S. 40 meets SR 1, turn left and head south to Connersville. Beyond Cambridge City, an old stone quarry on the left has filled with water. You'll cruise through Milton on Central Avenue, soon to see the countryside again with its cornfields and roadside stands.

Connersville, named for a fur trader, was only a trading post early in the 1800s, but in its heyday it thrived, turning out buggies, wagons, barrels, and other necessities. Located on the early Whitewater Canal, Connersville also got the railroad. Early in the twentieth century, the town began making automobiles, and at one time 10 different kinds of cars were made here.

In Connersville, SR 1 angles sharply left at West Thirtieth Street, turns south on Park Avenue along Roberts Park, skirts the downtown, and continues southeast. Stay on SR 1 and wind through rolling farmland. Horses graze in green pastures with white wooden fences. You can get local honey at a roadside stand. A weathered barn carries a faded ad for "Mail Pouch." During the Great Depression, the Mail Pouch Tobacco company used to provide paint if farmers would paint the name in bold letters beside the road. Continue through the Whitewater River valley past a large lake formed by a dam at Brookville.

Head west from Brookville on U.S. 52 to Metamora, and you'll pass Whitewater Valley Canoe Rental, Inc. These outfitters do a big business, offering 17 different trips over tranquil or white-water routes during an April-through-October season. One trip that is one to four hours long takes paddlers over parts of the old Whitewater Canal. Just before the Whitewater Canal State Historic Site, there's an attractive roadside park beside the old canal. Spread out your picnic here, and enjoy the canal without the crowds milling around in Metamora.

The Whitewater Canal, built between 1836 and 1847, ran from Lawrenceburg to Hagerstown, with a branch to Cincinnati. During this period, the Indiana government, with the help of federal money, also built the Wabash & Erie Canal in northern Indiana. The Whitewater Canal was used for transportation until 1860. A 15-mile stretch of the waterway, restored by the state, runs through Whitewater Canal State Historic Site at Metamora.

On the way into Metamora you'll notice this sign: "Where the past comes alive, the future is bright, and no one gets in a hurry." Park in one of the grassy lots so you can wander around at leisure. The town is a ramshackle wonder. Old wooden buildings, some accented with fieldstone, have become restaurants and stores. The Quilt Patch, an ice cream parlor, Rosebud Junction—in fact, dozens of stores—stand in rows along a loose grid of streets. More than a hundred shops operate here, mainly on weekends between May and October. At times, the scene resembles street theater. Metamora shops have more of a wild-West flavor than those in Brown County's Nashville (see Chapter 8). Shops sell everything from Italian sausage to delicate embroidery. Occasionally even tourists from Japan have found their way to Metamora's rough streets.

Watch from the bridge as the *Ben Franklin*, a colorful passenger barge pulled by draft horses, glides along the canal. Seated on the wooden deckhouse, the sightseers seem to be traveling in the nineteenth century. Except for Monday and Tuesday, the barge offers rides throughout the week.

Listen for the mellow whistle of an inbound train. When the railroad came in, the track to Metamora was laid on the old canal. Climb aboard the Whitewater Valley Railroad for a ride on a train pulled by steam engine. The 24-mile scenic route runs between Metamora and another depot in Connersville.

At the west end of Metamora, by Canal Lock No. 25, you'll discover the old Metamora Grist and Roller Mill. At the east end you'll see a rare covered bridge aqueduct, built in 1846 for canal boats.

Drive west on U.S. 52 from Metamora to cross the west fork of the Whitewater River. Turn left and go south on SR 229 toward Batesville, off the well-traveled routes. You'll pass through Peppertown, named for an early settler. Beyond, you'll go by small farms and orchards on the way to Oldenburg. From a distance, the hilltop spires rise above, resembling those of a village you'd find in Europe, not in southern

Indiana. Follow SR 229 through town, and you'll see the Immaculate Conception Convent to your right, beside a lovely chapel. Across the road, the steeple of the Holy Family Church, built in 1861, rises to 187 feet. In early times, settlers of German heritage settled the Whitewater Valley. Residents of Oldenburg have preserved this heritage: notice the street signs; they're *auf Deutsch*.

Continue south on SR 229 into Batesville, where the route ends at the landmark Sherman House Inn. Since 1852, the Sherman House, under various names, has catered to travelers. The original building included the present lobby, the Old Vienna Cafe, and the Sherman Lounge. In addition, the inn still offers guest rooms. On the restaurant menu, you'll find Hoosier fried chicken and lots of European dishes such as veal Oscar, beef burgundy, and sauerbraten. Dessert is always part of Hoosier hospitality, so allow yourself one of the inn's caloric delights.

For More Information

Wayne County Convention and Tourism Bureau (Richmond):
765-935-8687 or 800-828-8414

Hayes Regional Arboretum (Richmond): 765-962-3745

The Olde Richmond Inn (Richmond): 765-962-2247

Jag's Cafe (Centerville): 765-855-2282

Whitewater Valley Canoe Rental, Inc. (Brookville): 765-647-5434

Whitewater Canal State Historic Site (Metamora): 765-647-6512

Whitewater Valley Bicycle Route (map from Indiana State Parks):
800-622-4931

The Sherman House Inn (Batesville): 812-934-2407

8

Traipsing Around Hills & Hollows

Oliver Winery to Bean Blossum

Getting there: From Indianapolis, take SR 37 southwest to Bloomington. From Chicago, take I-80/90 and I-65 to I-465 west of Indianapolis. Exit on SR 37 and travel southwest to Bloomington. From Columbus, Ohio, take I-70 west to I-465. Drive south on I-465, exit at SR 37, and go southwest to Bloomington.

Highlights: sample Indiana wines, visit an art museum, or attend a concert; bike along country roads, shop in country stores, and rest on a bench with the locals.

The Oliver Winery, north of Bloomington, grew from a hobby gone awry. Three decades ago, Indiana University (I.U.) law professor Bill Oliver Sr. made wine as a hobby. Although Oliver and other Hoosier winemakers wanted to sell what they made, Indiana law didn't provide for small winery sales. They changed the law.

Drive to the Oliver Winery today, on SR 37, seven miles north of Bloomington, to see how this man's hobby has grown. You can visit the new tasting room and a vast warehouse, built in traditional post-and-beam style, using massive oak timbers. Since becoming Indiana's first winery in 1972, Oliver Wine Company, Inc., has also become Indiana's largest. The Oliver Winery has a reputation for Camelot mead (made with honey) and for medal-winning whites—sauvignon blanc, Gewürztraminer, and chenin blanc. They also make a subtle, fruity "Bean Blossum Blush," named for a nearby creek.

The Olivers have always made wine shopping fun, and you'll find meats, cheeses, crackers, and preserves in the gift shop, as well as wines. The dozen or so picnic tables scattered on the hillside invite you to stay. Below the grassy slope, a tranquil pond mirrors the foliage of the woodland.

After frolicking at the winery, tell your designated driver to head south on SR 37 to Bloomington. Exit at College Avenue (business route 37), and stop at the visitors' center on the right. There you can get maps of Bloomington, Monroe County, lakes, marinas, campgrounds, and forest preserves.

Continue south. At Fifteenth Street and College Avenue, the Butler Winery operates (since 1983) in an 80-year-old house. If time allows, they'll show you the cellar where wines are fermented, aged, and bottled. Sample some in the outdoor wine garden or in an indoor booth. Winemaker Jim Butler uses French grapes grown in southern Indiana vineyards: Seyval Blanc, Vidal, Vignoles, Chelois, and DeChaunac, along with eastern Concord and Niagara grapes. He makes a labor-intensive champagne-method sparkling wine as well, hand turning each bottle.

South on College Avenue is Bloomington's town square and the Monroe County Courthouse. In 1826, an early resident made the fish weathervane on this limestone building for the original courthouse. Around the historic square, sporting goods stores, book shops, and restaurants cater to the Indiana University campus population with choices ranging from exotic boutiques to a formal Chinese dining room. The Malibu Grill has very good food. The Bloomington Antique Mall (Sixth and Morton) has more than a hundred dealers under one roof. The parking garage at Fourth and Walnut Streets has a skywalk to the Fountain Square Mall, which features fine clothing, unique toy, and other specialty stores.

At the corner of Walnut and Kirkwood Streets, look east to see the gates of Indiana University's main campus. Drive east and you'll pass Ladyman's Cafe, the vintage Indiana Theater, a record store, and the Von Lee art movie house. The streetside People's Park is run by the city of Bloomington.

Lodging options in Bloomington include the Grant Street Inn at 310 North Grant Street, where two vintage Queen Anne homes have been joined by a breakfast room and deck. Each of the 24 rooms is decorated with antiques and has its own bath. Stay on a weeknight for lower rates. The Scholars Inn (801 North College Avenue) features five uniquely decorated rooms in an elegantly restored mansion—and serves gourmet breakfasts.

The city has grown in tandem with the university. It's also become a bicycling Mecca. Stay alert for two-wheelers, and be ready to brake for pedestrians.

At the end of Kirkwood Street, turn north onto Indiana Avenue. At Seventh Street, turn right and go east to see casually clad students relaxing. Some toss Frisbees or footballs while others stroll across the bridges over the Jordan River—which is actually a little creek. Despite the university's size, the heart of the campus still looks like countryside. The Indiana University student union, the largest in the world, sprawls on three levels in this wooded setting. At the east end, a hotel with bellhop service offers 190 guest rooms. You'll also find formal and informal restaurants, a courtyard, a bowling alley, a bakery, bookstores, guest parking lots, and other services.

Check the Union bulletin boards for information about folk dancing or stargazing. On weekday afternoons student volunteers lead campus walking tours. Call for information. Because of the university, Bloomington has an amazing choice of cultural activities. Beyond Showalter Fountain, at the end of Seventh Street, a huge auditorium, scheduled to reopen in September 1999, attracts performers like Luciano Pavarotti and productions like *A Chorus Line*. North of the fountain, the Indiana University Art Museum has 30,000 objects from primitive works to Fauve paintings. Housed in an I. M. Pei building, the museum hosts monthly concerts, Friday evening lectures, a film series, and a Saturday morning story session.

Across the Jordan River you'll find the I.U. Musical Arts Center. I.U. Opera Theater performs here in a state-of-the-art facility. The Lilly Library on Fine Arts Plaza has a collection of books by Indiana authors, including an autographed manuscript of *Ben Hur*. I.U. Theater performs at two campus locations and the Brown County Playhouse in Nashville, Indiana.

After walking about the campus, return to Indiana Avenue at Seventh Street, turn right, and head north. You'll pass the Mathers Museum of World Cultures on your right.

Travel east on Tenth Street, past Crosstown Shopping Center. Drive east across the bypass, to pick up SR 45 (also called Unionville Road). Take this delightful scenic drive northeast toward Lake Lemon, keeping an eye out for bicycle riders. This area of Bloomington became a magnet for cyclers after the film *Breaking Away*, a story about the annual Little 500 bicycle race. During the Hilly Hundred in autumn and the Hoosier Hills tours in spring, pedalers come from all over to ride here. Unfortunately, the rural roads have narrow shoulders and few separate bike lanes. So give bicyclists a full four feet of space when passing them, and signal any intention to turn. Follow along with them and you might feel *you're* breaking away, too.

Along SR 45, you'll see signs for the studios of Monroe County artists and craftspeople. The route has much of neighboring Brown County's rural charm, like a narrow wooden bridge and an old saltbox home with a white picket fence. In New Unionville, check out the shops for antiques and quilts.

Beyond New Unionville, ignore the turnoffs for Young and Skirkin Roads, but turn left on Tunnel Road and go north to Riddle Point Park on Lake Lemon's shore. This 1,650-acre lake, formed by damming Bean Blossom Creek, has become a haven for boat lovers. Surrounded by ridges, ravines, and forests, the lake has over 25 miles of shoreline. You can rent a canoe or rowboat near the swimming beach at Riddle Point Park. In summer, sailboats from the Lake Lemon Marina skim across the water. Near Salmon Harbor on the south shore, flocks of migrating waterfowl appear in spring and fall. In winter, people go ice skating, fishing, or cross-country skiing in the park.

When you've unwound at Riddle Point Park, drive south over Tunnel Road to South Shore Drive. Take the first road left and drive east along Lake Lemon's south shore. The road skirts rippled silky water and even crosses an embankment between the lake and a sheltered lagoon. Marshes thick with cattails support wildlife and shore birds, part of the Hoosier country scene.

At Trevlac, rejoin SR 45 and drive east through Helmsburg to Bean Blossom. At Helmsburg, you can shop for mops—or brooms, bentwood furniture, paintings, or crafts—at the Cullem Broom and Mop Factory.

From Bean Blossom, take the paved road southwest at the crossroads and you can drive through the Bean Blossom covered bridge. This is the only covered bridge actually built in the county; others were brought in. Built in 1880, the bridge has a rustic setting favored by artists and photographers.

You'll see lots of Brown County hills and hollows, formed by receding glaciers as the Ice Age was ending. The Illinois Glacier came into the region just north of Bean Blossom. As it melted, the runoff became streams and formed hollows, giving Brown County this rugged terrain.

Continue south on this road to reach SR 135, the road to Nashville. Just north of the junction, stop for a great scenic view at Bean Blossom Overlook, a roadside rest park. Continue south on SR 135 to Nashville, the county seat of Brown County, and you'll pass many artists' homes, including a log cabin that once belonged to Marie Goth.

Brown County could well be the country roads capital of Indiana. Named for war hero Jacob J. Brown, the county drew settlers who found the land difficult to farm, so they turned to logging and salt mining. In 1875, some began mining the hills for gold, though quantities were never found. Residents today have a gold mine in tourism.

Soon after arriving, find the *Brown County Almanac* in one of the local shops, and peruse the information about the restaurants, museums, and stores here. The Nashville Chamber of Commerce on Van Buren Street has a good map of Nashville streets and the intricate network of county roads.

Despite the people milling about Van Buren and Main Streets, and the surfeit of shops and restaurants, Nashville is still fun. Yet at night it's so quiet you can hear the raccoons rattling residents' trash cans as they sample the leavings. For entertainment, catch a performance at the Brown County Playhouse, or hear a country music star down the road at the Little Nashville Opry House.

Notice the log buildings along Van Buren Street and on the north side of East Main Street. There are 50 such buildings in Nashville and maybe 450 throughout the county. The *Brown County Lodging Guide*, available from the Nashville Chamber of Commerce, lists 15 log cabins you can rent; one is more than a hundred years old.

Bed and breakfasts also flourish in Nashville and its environs, combining service with distinctive decoration. The Allison House Inn has a central location, unique decor, and a lavish breakfast. Other choices are a historic farm, an A-frame cottage, a three-story chalet, a large house, a Victorian home, and even a restored general store.

The Hob Nob Corner Restaurant, at the corner of Main and Van Buren Streets in a former general store, serves good sandwiches and salads in a dining area half hidden by a gift shop. Built during the early 1870s, the Hob Nob could well be the oldest commercial building in the county.

Over 300 art galleries, antique stores, and craft and specialty shops now line Van Buren and Main going east toward Greasy Creek. Shops beside shops and within shops sell paintings, sculpture, stained glass, handcrafted wood furniture, carvings, pewterware, toys, jewelry, clothing, and home decorations. At studio shops, you can watch craftspeople at work in traditional fashion, making pottery, blowing glass, or weaving.

The Nashville House, at the corner of Van Buren and Main Streets, traces its history back to 1859. Loggers, artists, and travelers stayed in this wooden hostelry at the crossroads. In 1927, entrepreneurs remodeled and built onto the original structure and touted home cooking and special fried biscuits. After the building burned in 1943, owner Jack Rogers put up a new rustic building, and the inn became a restaurant. Now the dining tables are hidden behind gadgets in the Old Country Store. The heavy fare—fried chicken, roast turkey, home-baked breads, Hoosier ham, barbecued ribs—can be a real country experience. They even have sassafras tea. Before you leave, note the fascinating photo gallery of old-time residents on the south wall of the Nashville House lobby.

South of the Nashville House on Van Buren Street you'll find the Ordinary, a pub-style restaurant. It serves corned-beef, vegetarian, wild-game, and other sandwiches and dinners centering around fish, fowl, and beef. For authentic regional cuisine, try the "Wild Game Feast," featuring pheasant and turkey.

Across the street from the Ordinary, the Brown County Playhouse, Indiana's longest-running professional summer theater, celebrated its 50th year in 1998. The small, rustic theater presents musicals, comedies, and serious plays throughout the season. Actor Kevin Kline and writer/producer Howard Ashman (*Beauty and the Beast*) are among the distinguished alumni of the Brown County Playhouse.

Nearby, the Liar's Benches on the lawn of the brick courthouse have an interesting history. The original bench, provided by a local merchant, allowed people to "set a spell" and swap stories. As the number of storytellers grew over the years, so did the number of benches.

Don't miss the buildings in the Brown County Historical Society complex at the corner of Gould Street and Old School Way. The Settler's Cabin, brought from Jackson County, dates from the 1840s. Dr. Ralphy's office holds the medical practitioner's old books, instruments, and furniture. The Old Log Jail, a two-story structure with double walls, was built for maximum security.

Four blocks east of the courthouse on Main Street at Artist Drive, the Brown County Art Gallery displays work of local artists, some of whom are quite well regarded. Drawn by the area's peaceful rural ambience, artist T. C. Steele launched the artists' migration to Brown County in 1907.

Around Nashville, you'll see drawings of Abe Martin, a cartoon character who "resided" in Brown County. Created by Frank McKinney "Kin" Hubbard, the drawings entertained newspaper readers with their rural wisdom between 1904 and 1930.

Beyond Nashville, scenic country roads run in every direction. Take SR 46 southwest toward Belmont, for instance, and you'll drive past the Little Nashville Opry House (located about a mile from town). Though it's not Branson, Missouri, Little Nashville does host country music performers in a 1,700-seat auditorium.

Down the road a piece (three more miles), you'll see the Schooner Valley Stables, Inc. Open year-round, they offer scenic trail rides for various ages and experience levels. Rides range from one to three hours in length, through beautiful countryside. Ask about the moonlight rides, horse-drawn hayrides, stagecoach rides, and in winter, rides on a horse-drawn sleigh.

Continue on SR 46 through Belmont another mile and a half to the T. C. Steele State Historic Site. The artist Theodore Clement Steele built a home called the House of Singing Winds on this site in 1907. Notice several hiking trails that meander through the 211-acre estate. The artist's 11-room house contains many of his impressionist paintings, and you'll see two studios where he worked and a large collection of books. T. C. Steele and his wife believed that "here in this hill country" the special character of the outdoors would "bring out their finest spirit"—an interesting philosophy.

After visiting the estate, continue south on Dewar Ridge Road to Lake Monroe. The water sprawls over 10,750 acres from the eastern boundary of Brown County southwest almost to Harrodsburg. Conceived as a flood-control project, the lake has become the largest body of water in the state. Much of Lake Monroe's shoreline winds through Hoosier National Forest lands. Along the shore are recreational areas, private resorts, marinas, and campgrounds.

Stay on the road as it curves northeast and becomes Crooked Creek Road. You'll pass Ault Lake and complete a loop back to SR 46. Turn right at the highway and go northeast. Before returning to Nashville, you can enter Brown County State Park at the west gate; pick up a map at the gatehouse. Otherwise, continue on SR 46 *through* Nashville, and

T. C. Steele State Historic Site

enter at the north (main) gate. You'll pass the two-lane Ramp Creek Covered Bridge, one of the oldest covered bridges in Indiana.

Brown County State Park, Indiana's largest, contains 15,547 acres with hiking trails and bridle paths, two lakes, a nature center, tennis courts, and a swimming pool. Small creeks cut through ravines below forested hills awash with bluish haze. For a panoramic view, climb the fire tower on Weed Patch Hill. Near the north entrance, the popular Abe Martin Lodge and Restaurant draws crowds of visitors during peak autumn foliage time. In fact, the scenic park draws more than two million visitors every year.

After exploring the park, exit North Park Entrance and go east on SR 46 to Salt Creek Road, just beyond the KOA Campground. Turn left and drive northeast along a fork of Salt Creek toward Gatesville, wandering the country roads away from tourist attractions. You'll pass year-round country homes whose residents, for entertainment, watch an occasional opossum cross the road.

Brown County's rural villages, Gatesville, Story, Bean Blossom, and others, each center around a country store. There's usually a church nearby, supported by rural residents. At Gatesville, turn left at the paved Bean Blossom/Gatesville Road, drive west past the Goshen Church, and you'll see Bear Wallow Hill on the left. The Indians who once hunted and fished this region found a wealth of game, including bears. Continue on the road beside Bean Blossom Creek. Some historians trace this name to a Miami Indian word. Others say Bean Blossom was a man who nearly drowned trying to swim the creek in 1812. Continue west and you'll be back in Bean Blossom, the end of the drive.

Brown County—where more people live out in the forest than in Nashville town—reveals itself slowly, so plan to come again.

For More Information

All numbers are within area code 812 unless otherwise noted.

Oliver Winery (Bloomington): 876-5800 or 800-258-2783

Bloomington/Monroe County Convention and Visitors' Bureau (Bloomington): 334-8900 or 800-800-0037

Butler Winery (Bloomington): 339-7233

Fourth Street Festival of the Arts and Crafts (Bloomington/ Monroe County Convention and Visitors' Bureau; Bloomington): 334-8900 or 800-800-0037

Grant Street Inn (Bloomington): 334-2353 or 800-328-4350

Scholars Inn (Bloomington): 332-1892 or 800-765-3466

Indiana University Memorial Union (Bloomington): 856-6381 or 800-209-8145

Indiana University Campus Walking Tours (Bloomington): 855-0661

Indiana University Auditorium (box office, handles I.U. Theater; Bloomington): 855-1103

Indiana University Art Museum (Bloomington): 855-5445

Indiana University Opera Theater/Musical Arts Center (box office; Bloomington): 855-7433

Mathers Museum (Bloomington): 855-6873

Brown County Convention and Visitors' Bureau (Nashville): 988-7303 or 800-753-3255

The Nashville House (Nashville): 988-4554

Bellflower Shop (Nashville): 988-4964

Brown County Playhouse (box office; Nashville): 988-2123

Schooner Valley Stables, Inc. (Nashville): 988-2859

T. C. Steele State Historic Site (Nashville): 988-2785

Indiana Wine Grape Council (winery information): 317-481-0222 or 800-832-WINE

9

Discovering Quarries & Caves

Bedford to Milltown

Getting there: From Indianapolis, take SR 37 southwest to Bedford. From Chicago, take I-80/90 and I-65 to I-465 west of Indianapolis. Exit on SR 37 and drive southwest to Bedford. From Columbus, Ohio, take I-70 west to I-465. Drive south and west to exit on SR 37. Continue southwest to Bedford.

Highlights: explore a village where tourists never go and travel by boat on an underground river; visit a cemetery with famous carvings, enjoy dogwoods in bloom in the spring, or go to the Persimmon Festival in the fall.

Bedford limestone has long played a major architectural role in America. You can find it in the Empire State Building in New York, on an old residence in Miami Beach, and in the Biltmore Mansion near Asheville, North Carolina.

Drive west from downtown Bedford along Sixteenth Street and note the various uses of stone. Stone facings embellish the wood frame houses. Stone pillars support front porch roofs. Stone walls mark property lines. Welcome to "Stone City," a town that thrived at the turn of the century with the demand for Indiana limestone.

During the great boom, 39 stone mills operated in the Bedford area and 4,000 men worked with great blocks of stone cut from 32 different quarries. Skilled stone carvers using mallets and chisels prepared the detailed statues and friezes desired by architects of the period.

Drive on west of Bedford via SR 158, about three miles west of SR 37, to visit Elliott Special Products (ESP), Inc. Phone ahead and guides will take you through an aboveground quarry. They'll tell you how the limestone was formed and about the way natural forces exposed bedrock in the Bedford area. Started by four women in 1989, ESP has a gift shop with handcrafted limestone coasters, bookends, and alphabet letters.

From the ESP showroom, continue west along SR 158 past the Shiloh Cemetery and through Fayetteville, named for an early settler. West of Fayetteville, turn left on CR 650 west, a paved road. The route winds through pastureland and cornfields in scenic limestone country. Ramble uphill through a tunnel of trees down into a roller-coaster dip. Turn onto a T-road (90 degrees to the right), and you'll enter the Hoosier National Forest. The road curves southwest and eventually becomes CR 900. Fortunately, just before deciding you're hopelessly lost, you'll arrive in the town of Williams.

Perched on a hilltop above a popular fishing lake, Williams is that rare country community where people don't do a thing to attract tourists. Up the road from the Williams Bait and Tackle Shop, you'll see a square, two-story brick building,

Pinnick's Country Store. Here, old-timers pull up benches to wooden tables and talk about their neighbors over mugs of iced tea. Stocked floor to ceiling with groceries, it's a good source of picnic supplies. Stroll downhill to see the dam, a vintage Williams Milling Company building, and public rest rooms. From an open deck, you can watch water tumble and boil into a muddy froth below. The dam, a flood-control project, has formed a lake from a fork of the White River.

From Williams, take SR 450 west of town. Turn left and go south under a wooden railroad trestle toward the river. Built in 1884, this 402-foot-long covered bridge is the longest such tunnel still used in Indiana.

Go east on SR 450 back through town and around the edge of the lake, then turn onto an unmarked road beyond marshy ponds on the right. Follow this road east for a lovely sweeping valley view that is particularly gorgeous in the fall. Continue on this road until you cross the river. Take the next road right (a red house stands at the corner). Follow CR 500 west to CR 450 south and watch for the Bluespring Caverns sign.

One of the world's 10 largest, Bluespring Caverns has an underground river flowing through it fed by miles of subterranean streams. Called the Myst'ry River, the waters eventually join the White River downstream. Open to the public since 1971, this cave system wasn't discovered until the 1940s, when a farmer awoke one morning after heavy rains to find an opening to the cave where his farm pond had been the day before.

At Bluespring Caverns, you can take an hour-long boat ride on the Myst'ry River. Notice the cave's rough surfaces mirrored on the dark water. Especially during the first part of the tour, you'll see stalactites, flowstones, and drapery formations. Lights from the boat reveal craggy limestone formations and create deep shadows resembling those the first cave visitors must have seen.

Pale, blind fish and almost colorless crayfish inhabit the cavern, and sometimes fish from above-ground streams wander in. Although the boat only travels about a mile and a quarter through the cave, there are more than 20 miles of known passageways.

After touring Bluespring Caverns, take CR 450 south to U.S. 50. Drive north on U.S. 50 and return to Bedford. This route becomes M Street, an avenue dividing Bedford's east and west sides. Turn right on Eighteenth Street for the entrance to Green Hill Cemetery.

Looping roads wind around the grassy, well-kept cemetery, so a few famous stones can be seen on a drive-through. Better yet, park outside the gates and look around on foot. Over the years, the Green Hill burial ground has become a showcase for Bedford's legendary carvers, and some monuments have been shown on national television. Even people who don't care that much for cemeteries can admire the stonecutters' work. The oldest stones cluster in the northeast quadrant where there are no roads. Here are monuments to leading nineteenth-century townspeople: businesspeople, attorneys, doctors, journalists, and stonecutters.

Notice the tree-trunk carvings, a very popular style. On one such memorial, branches from a deceased couple's stones have been intertwined. Angels with wings were also popular and were most often used on a child's grave.

Walk up the hill to find the famous stonecutter monuments, on both sides of the road east of the circle. These carvings capture facial expressions, body postures, the texture of fabric, the folds in cloth. An immigrant carver with his tools inspired the Stonecutter's Memorial. The workbench carving is a tribute to stonecutter Lewis Baker, created by fellow stonecutters. The monument resembles Baker's workbench the way he left it on the day he died.

From the cemetery, drive two blocks north along M Street. There you'll find a restaurant (beside the Mark III Motel on the left) where locals find good—though not very spicy—Mexican food. When you reach Sixteenth Street (U.S. 50), turn right to go east through downtown Bedford.

The two-story Lawrence County Building (on Sixteenth Street between I and J Streets) squats low and uses high-placed urns for decoration. In the basement, the Lawrence County Historical Society Museum collection has 5,000 items and is well worth a stop.

Continue on U.S. 50 east of town to Otis Park, donated to Bedford by a newspaperman. The golf course has a creek running through it and an old brick mansion beside the road. Veer right on Tunnelton Road and drive southeast past Virgil Grissom Municipal Airport. One of the "Gemini Seven" in the 1960s, astronaut Grissom pioneered in space exploration and became a national hero, yet the folks in his home county remember him simply as "Gus."

Beyond the airport, turn right onto CR 250 south and drive to U.S. 50/SR 37. Turn left and follow SR 37 south toward Mitchell. Along the way, you'll see five smaller cemeteries with distinctive carved stones like those at Green Hill. Watch for Applacres signs about four miles south. This well-stocked open market has an array of produce—even persimmons— in season. A persimmon is a tart, seedy fruit that falls from its tree as it ripens, and many Lawrence County people grow them.

Northwest of Mitchell, take old SR 37 into town. Beyond the cemetery, turn left and follow Main Street into the central part of the city; notice all the antique shops! Time it right, and you can visit Mitchell during the September Persimmon Festival. For more than four decades, Mitchell has held a fall festival that gets bigger every year. During the hoopla, Main Street between Fifth and Eighth Streets becomes a midway with booths, rides, displays, and food stands. Hot-air balloons drift above the trees, and brightly clad marching bands strut through downtown streets. Along with the Persimmon Festival Queen, the community also recognizes the creative cook who makes the best persimmon pudding. Check out the local grocery stores, and you'll usually find persimmon pulp with the canned goods or cartons of frozen pulp in the freezer.

On a farm west of Mitchell, Dymple Green (her real name), who judged the pudding contest for 12 years, produces "Dymple's Delight" canned persimmon pulp. Using stainless-steel equipment, she strains out the seeds and cans the pulp in a remodeled pony barn behind her home. "We have a tremendous mail order business," Green says, aligning the cartons of canned pulp stacked for tomorrow's shipment. She puts her mother's pudding recipe on the orange label of each can and has published recipes she's collected over the years.

At the corner of Brook and Seventh Streets, a renovated opera house has made the *National Register of Historic Places*. Built originally with state funds, the opera house drew early Mitchell residents in for vaudeville shows. It was closed for years, until a student and other community leaders launched a drive to restore it; people came from miles around to help. Now bluegrass, country music, Dixieland, and pop classic groups once again offer live entertainment.

At Main and Sixth Streets, turn south and drive past the Grissom Memorial near the corner of Grissom Avenue. Virgil "Gus" Grissom had a home on this street. Continue south on Sixth Street to SR 60. Turn left and drive east to Spring Mill State Park, a Hoosier favorite with its homey lodge, miles of scenic hiking and bridle trails, reconstructed pioneer village and working gristmill, and several caves. Since 1971, people have also come to visit the Grissom Memorial. Park on the right near the main entrance.

During the 1950s and 1960s, Lawrence County residents avidly tracked Grissom's career as the small-town Mitchell boy who married his high school sweetheart and became a national hero. After a history-making suborbital flight in 1961, Grissom splashed down at sea, only to lose the space capsule. Even so, NASA learned much from the experience, and honors were heaped on Grissom. As command pilot of the first manned flight of the Gemini series, he had orbited the Earth three times in space capsule *Molly Brown*. Tragically, Grissom and two other astronauts died in a launch pad accident at Cape Kennedy in 1967. In the memorial at Spring Mill, you can examine Grissom's space suit and the *Gemini III* space capsule.

East of the park, Trail No. 3 links several caves and passes through virgin timber in Donaldson Woods Nature Preserve. During the Autumn Harvest Days celebration in October, peak foliage time, Spring Mill holds nature hikes, demonstrations of pioneer crafts, and old-time contests like sack races.

From the park, take CR 300 east opposite the park entrance. Then turn right and take CR 1050 south, and you'll reach SR 37. Turn left and go south toward Orleans, the Dogwood Capital of Indiana and the oldest town in Orange County. Since the 1960s, people here have planted hundreds of these flowering trees along roads and parks and in their own backyards. If possible, come in springtime to see the trees in bloom. The town centers around Seminary Square, named for an academy that operated here for nearly a century.

South of Orleans, continue on SR 37 and you'll find the Lost River—or at least the dry riverbed. The creek starts flowing in Washington County, then winds west above and below ground for about 22 miles. After it passes under the road south of Orleans, it joins the east fork of the White River downstream. The dry channel beneath the bridge sometimes carries runoff after heavy rains.

As the road drops into a picturesque valley, SR 37 passes the Paoli town square and the photogenic courthouse. This Greek revival structure has a stately colonnaded portico and iron staircases running up and down the back. On the south side, the three-story Landmark Hotel operated from the late 1800s to the mid-twentieth century. Paoli (as well as West Baden and French Lick) lies in the heart of Hoosier mineral-spa country, where people once came to "take the waters." Brought by their desire for better health, they came to bathe in mineral springs and get the supposed benefits of bottled waters.

From Paoli, take SR 56 west/U.S. 150 to Prospect. Continue south on SR 56 at Prospect to West Baden Springs. As you drive near, look for the top of the old West Baden Springs Hotel, known for its enormous unsupported dome, the world's third largest. The hotel, currently being renovated, was once a playground for the rich and not-so-famous. At one time, guests could play golf, gamble in a casino, go bicycle or horseback riding, watch ponies run a track, and enjoy live shows in the opera house.

Drive through West Baden on SR 56, and you'll see an old depot on the right, now a railway museum. Among the array of old locomotives and cars is a rare post office car. Climb aboard the French Lick, West Baden & Southern train for a scenic ride through Hoosier forests and beneath limestone cliffs. The train goes through the 2,200-foot Burton tunnel before returning to the station, a former Monon Railroad depot. The season for these rides runs from April through November.

Just beyond the depot, the French Lick Springs Hotel, Golf, and Tennis Resort boasts a colorful history. The first hotel here opened in 1840, and although some people thought it ugly, the destination proved popular. The coming of the railroad gave the resort another boost, but popularity later declined. In 1902, when the place was in ruins, an Indianapolis mayor and entrepreneur bought it. With additional development, the resort drew notables at the beginning of the twentieth century. Chef Louis Perrin oversaw the kitchen, which turned out memorable food. John Barrymore, Clark Gable, and Bing Crosby were all guests at French Lick, as were the presidential Roosevelts, Trumans, and Reagans. Today, the resort caters to families, who come to ski at nearby Paoli Peak.

Across the road, the former Pluto water-bottling plant promoted its product with the slogan, "If Nature won't, Pluto will!"—a reference to the water's laxative properties.

From French Lick, drive south on SR 145 to Eckerty. This route winds through Hoosier National Forest land and crosses a bridge at Patoka Lake, a popular recreation area formed by a dam. At Eckerty, turn left and drive east via SR 64 through Taswell and English. Some of these small Crawford County towns were passed by when the railroads came. Nearly half the county is covered with forest, mainly in national and state reserves. The area's hilltop vistas, hidden streams and valleys, and fascinating caves mean future potential for tourism. Locals enjoy an outdoor lifestyle, going camping, boating, hunting, and fishing.

Continue east on SR 64 to Marengo, where a U.S. national landmark cavern, Marengo Cave Park, offers tours year-round. In 1883, some students at the Marengo Academy found an opening to the cave and started planning to explore it. While working in the academy kitchen, a 15-year-old girl overheard their talk, and taking her younger brother along, she entered the cave ahead of the others. The farmer who owned the property lost no time in making it a public attraction. The Crystal Palace Tour, which takes less than an hour, is a favorite of many visitors. It involves walking through cavernous rooms filled with elaborate, dripping decorations and watching a pageant. The Dripstone Trail Tour, over an hour in length, features a walk past delicate soda-straw formations and totem-pole stalagmites. The Crystal Palace has been open to the public for more than a century. The Dripstone Trail opened in 1979.

In the scenic woodland surrounding these caverns, you'll find a nature trail and areas for swimming, hiking, fishing, and horseback riding.

After exploring Marengo Cave Park, go west on SR 64, to the turnoff at Milltown. Here the Cave Country Canoes, an adventure center, has pumped life into a slumbering mill town. Wrap up your drive through Indiana limestone country with a canoe trip along the Blue River. Even beginners can handle the seven-mile Totten Ford trip. Paddle downstream past scenic bluffs, and you'll see old lime kilns and quarries and even paddle a few light rapids. The 14-mile Rothrock Mill trip, with best water levels between March and July, takes much of the day, but the rewards are major. Towering limestone cliffs rise to the sky. Rapids, chutes, and flumes lie waiting. And at the finish, you'll discover the old Rothrock Dam and Mill. Paddling these waters, you may recall the challenges faced by early explorers traveling uncharted waters in birchbark canoes.

For More Information

All numbers are within area code 812.

Bedford Chamber of Commerce: 275-4493

Elliott Stone Company, Inc. (Bedford): 275-5556

Elliott Special Products, Inc. (Bedford): 275-1900

Hoosier National Forest (Bedford): 275-5987

Mark III Motel (Bedford): 275-5935

Applacres, Inc. (Bedford): 279-9721

Greater Mitchell Chamber of Commerce (Persimmon Festival; Mitchell): 849-4441

Opera House (Mitchell): 849-2337

Spring Mill Inn (Mitchell): 849-4081

Spring Mill State Park (Mitchell): 849-4129

French Lick Springs Hotel (French Lick): 936-9300

Cave Country Canoes (Milltown): 633-4993

10

Wandering the Lincoln Trail

Huntingburg to Corydon

Getting there: From Indianapolis, take SR 37 southwest to I-64; drive west on I-64 to SR 45, then north to Huntingburg.

Highlights: see *The Young Lincoln* drama and the Lincoln family farm; mail letters at the Santa Claus post office; visit a monastery, explore more caves, and walk around historic Corydon.

At the Fourth Street Deli, locals have never met a carbohydrate they didn't like. They can resist anything but temptation. Reuben sandwiches, turkey and pastrami, braunschweiger, and salami highlight the menu. Desserts are "fat man's delights." If you're not served in five minutes, you'll get served in eight or nine, maybe twelve, the kitchen explains. You can relax in Huntingburg.

Stroll along Fourth Street, just outside the door, to browse among the antique, handicraft, and specialty stores on Huntingburg's main street. The stores aren't crowded, and the shopkeepers will even talk to you. No one is pushing for a sale.

The town's founder decided to stay around because he liked hunting game, everything from pigeons to bears. Between 1908 and 1944, Uhl Pottery made bricks and other items here, using natural clay dug from the nearby hills. While other towns grew rapidly, Huntingburg couldn't afford to raze the old buildings to put up new ones, so many of the handsome brick structures still stand today.

From the corner of Fourth and Geiger Streets, walk south half a block to see the town's Italianate firehouse. Built in 1887, the Huntingburg Town Hall and Fire Engine House has walls 14 inches thick and distinctive second-floor windows.

From the heart of Huntingburg, take U.S. 231 south through Dale toward Gentryville. South of Dale, Little Pigeon Creek flows through forests and cornfields. Continue on U.S. 231 to Gentryville, and at the sign for Jones House State Historic Site, turn right and go west (less than a mile) to the former home of William Jones, a prominent early citizen. Jones lived in a cabin and operated a trading post here while Abraham Lincoln was growing up. At one time, young Abe worked for him in the store. A lifelong friend, Jones became a colonel and a hero during the War Between the States. After Jones built this Federal-style brick residence in 1835, Lincoln visited him while campaigning for Henry Clay.

Return to Gentryville, named for early settlers, and head east on SR 162—a designated scenic highway—at the sign for Lincoln Parks. On the left, a sign will direct you to the site of the early Gentry house. Continue east through lovely wooded forest land, and you'll soon come to the entrance to Lincoln State Park, on the right. Besides the usual facilities, this park contains an amphitheater where *The Young Lincoln* musical drama takes place. Billy Edd Wheeler's story, produced by the University of Southern Indiana, narrates the Lincoln years in Indiana, including a flatboat trip downriver. If you hike the Noah Gordon Trail (it branches off Trail 1—get a trail map at the park entrance), you'll hike by the Noah Gordon mill site where Lincoln used to have his grain ground. You'll also pass the grave of Lincoln's only sister, Sarah Lincoln Grigsby, and a Baptist church built near the site of the church the Lincolns attended.

Return to SR 162 east. On the left, the Lincoln Boyhood National Memorial, run by the National Park Service, has three main areas. Visit the memorial building first, for background. The Lincolns came to Indiana in 1816, the year the territory became a state. Nancy Hanks Lincoln died just two years later, when Abe was nine. Over the years, her grave has become a memorial park, just a short walk up to a wooded knoll from the Lincoln memorial. After visiting the gravesite, drive west of the memorial, turn right, and go north on the central park road to the Lincoln farm. With its log cabin, sheds, animals, gardens, and fields bounded by split-rail fences, it gives you insight into the lifestyle of the Lincolns and other pioneers.

Return to the entrance of the Lincoln Boyhood National Memorial. Continue east on SR 162 to the Santa Claus post office, in a stone castle on the left, beside Holiday World. Handy drive-up boxes take your mail to be postmarked when the post office is closed. Established in 1856, the post office grew in volume of mail handled, but a large town never developed here. By 1967 the town had 2,358 acres and only 31 residents. But the growth in mail transactions was something else. During the late 1920s, the Santa Claus postmaster began answering children's letters to Santa and stamping the Santa Claus postmark on an increasing volume of mail. Now each year as Christmas approaches, mail comes in from countries around the world. Senders in foreign countries enclose International Reply Coupons to pay for the stamps. People in the community pitch in to help, signing letters and folding and stuffing them into decorated envelopes to be mailed from zip code 47579—the town of Santa Claus.

Over the years, several theme parks have operated on the land behind the post office. Since 1980, Holiday World has become even larger and better, boasting dozens of rides, musical shows, gift shops, and several museums.

Continue on SR 162 to the left of the post office; the route curves north. At SR 62, turn right and drive toward St. Meinrad, where a Benedictine monastery, college, and seminary share a lovely hilltop location. St. Meinrad was a young Benedictine monk who left a Swiss monastery in the ninth century so he could live alone on Mount Etzel, where he built a shrine. While he lived, he attracted many visitors, including a band of robbers who killed him. The Swiss honor him as a martyr and saint.

The Abbey of Einsiedeln founded a monastery here in 1854 to serve the growing number of German immigrants in southern Indiana. To the right of the central abbey complex is a guest house (reservations suggested) and visitors' center. Ask for information on the self-guided tour. The Abbey Church is a Romanesque structure built of local sandstone. Marble statues above the entrance depict St. Benedict, St. Scholastica, and the Virgin Mary holding the boy Jesus. The Abbey Press has two plants on the campus and a gift shop a half mile from the guest house at the southeast corner of the abbey grounds. Follow the paved road west of the guest house.

After leaving the grounds, turn right on SR 62. To find the Shrine of Our Lady of Monte Cassino, drive east to the sign and go up the hill. More than a hundred years old, the chapel was built in this tranquil, wooded setting in gratitude for the first sandstone quarried here.

Continue east along SR 62, a scenic Ohio River valley road through rolling countryside and Hoosier National Forest land. Back in the woods there's a clubhouse for the Crawford

County Coon Hunters. Here and there on the right are wide vistas of the mighty Ohio River.

On the way into Leavenworth, Paul Tower and his wife, Norma, sell fresh produce at the Tower Orchard Market, located at the intersection of SRs 66 and 62. "Everything's home grown," Paul says. In season they have large Hoosier cantaloupes and watermelons, Madison peaches, tomatoes, squash, eggplant, hot and sweet peppers, corn, green beans, and cabbage. They also stock fruit preserves, honey, molasses, and apple butter—some of it locally made. Paul Tower was born and raised in a nearby farmhouse, one of 12 children, says Norma. Married 32 years, the Towers now run a business passed down from Paul's grandfather. At one time, they both worked in Louisville, but the Towers like country life. "We chose to come here," Norma explains.

Farther down the road, stop again at the Overlook Restaurant on the right. Perched on top of a bluff, the place has a great view of a horseshoe bend in the muddy Ohio River. The restaurant in this rambling white building has dining rooms on two levels, with many window views. The menu—with chicken and biscuits, Beef Manhattan, sliced baked ham, and the like—features dishes made by Hoosier country cooks for decades. Try the coconut cream pie.

An earlier Leavenworth, founded in 1818 by two cousins, once flourished in the bottoms. After a 1937 flood damaged or destroyed more than a hundred buildings, former residents sought higher ground and rebuilt the town in its present location atop a 400-foot bluff. Continue east on SR 62. One mile beyond the eastern limits of the new Leavenworth, a road leads off to the old town below. Drive on east of this turnoff a half mile to find Overlook Park, an appealing picnic ground with a great river view.

Continue traveling this scenic route until the road dips into a wooded valley. You'll suspect you're in cave country as rugged limestone cliffs rise above you on either side of the road. Indians in the area used Big Wyandotte Cave for shelter in prehistoric times and dug chert, argonite, and other compounds from its interior. Later, white settlers mined saltpeter and exomite here. The main use of the caves now is tourism.

Turn left at the sign to enter the Wyandotte Caves State Recreation Area; these caves contain some of the largest rooms and interior mountains in the United States. Big Wyandotte Cave has been open to visitors since the mid-nineteenth century, when businessman Henry P. Rothrock realized its commercial potential. Although it wasn't opened to the public until years later, Little Wyandotte Cave, 700 feet to the south, has been known since 1856, the year Rothrock opened a vacation lodge here. A New Albany newspaper once called Wyandotte "the world's greatest natural wonder." Later, an Evansville car dealer offered "expense paid" Wyandotte trips for two as an incentive to car buyers, who then drove their new roadsters to Wyandotte Lodge.

Today, tours of the caves are priced from $1.50 to $10.00 per adult and range from a 30-minute introduction to a strenuous effort lasting most of the day. Little Wyandotte, the shortest and easiest trip, offers a good overall view. The Historical Tour through Big Wyandotte includes a Rugged Mountain section early visitors never saw. The Monument Mountain Tour covers a mile and a half of steep terrain past rare formations and early quarries. The Pillar of the Constitution Tour involves four or five hours of walks, climbs, and crawls. To get into the upper passages of the Old Caves, you have to climb a wooden pole above an animal pit and squeeze through an opening called the Straits; if your chest measures more than 46 inches, best ask about another tour. The All Day Tour involves seven or eight hours of strenuous activity. Visitors see Milroy's Temple, crawl through Worm Alley, and go past Crawfish Springs. To enter Jones's Discovery, people with chests larger than 44 inches need not apply.

A network of interesting trails above the ground are sometimes overlooked by people who think the caves are all that's worth seeing. Four trails rank as rugged, five as moderate, and only the one to the fire tower is easy. Ask for a self-guided tour map, then follow the Twigs to Timber route and learn to identify 18 native Indiana trees. The rugged Adventure Trail, marked with green, leads to a scenic river overlook (and so does the road, SR 462).

Once you've finished exploring, return to the park entrance and take SR 62 east to Corydon. You can't miss the Red Barn, which overflows with antiques, table linens, patchwork quilts, old china, glassware, ancient tools, and furniture on three floors—more than 6,000 square feet in all.

SR 62 leads across Big Indian Creek and through central Corydon on Walnut Street. Because many of the early state government buildings have been restored, the downtown has become a mixture of historic buildings and private businesses. At the corner of Walnut and Elm Streets, stop at the information center for city and county maps. You may also want maps for self-guided tours of the historic buildings or the central shops and stores.

The Corydon Capital State Historic Site consists of all the buildings relating to state government here before 1825. The town became the seat of territorial government in 1813, and served as the state's first capital from 1816 to 1825. In the central square stands the two-story limestone building used by the early legislators. With its hip roof and cupola, it has been a state memorial since 1929. Workers restored the original flagstone floor, fireplaces and west door transom and used vintage hardware, railings, doors, and so forth to fashion much of the rest. With windows open and the breeze blowing through, you can almost see early government in action. During June of 1816, the building was still under construction when delegates gathered to write the new state's constitution. Because of the

First state capitol building, Corydon

summer heat, some groups met informally beneath a huge elm tree, later dubbed the Constitution Elm. Visit this memorial at the west end of High Street.

Many shops, such as the Indian Creek Trading Post, line the square along Chestnut Street. Across the street, find desserts, sandwiches, and ice cream. In the Griffin Building at 113 East Beaver Street, over 40 antiques dealers have small shops that are open six days a week plus Sunday afternoons. Sugarbabies (219 High Street) also has antiques, along with Norwegian furniture made to the buyer's specifications.

You'll find the depot for the 1883 Corydon Scenic Railroad at the corner of Walnut and Water Streets. The railroad came in long after Corydon's role in state government was history. Yet the network of rails has encouraged travel and commerce in Indiana, as have the canals, highways, and airfields. Climb aboard the Louisville, New Albany & Corydon (LNAC) Railroad train for an hour-and-a-half ride into the hills. As the uniformed conductor explains what you see, the nostalgic 16-mile journey takes you back to the nineteenth century.

For More Information

All numbers are within area code 812.

Fourth Street Deli (Huntingburg): 683-5650

Jones House State Historic Site (Gentryville): 937-2802

Lincoln State Park (Lincoln City): 937-4710

The Young Lincoln show (Lincoln City): 937-4493 or 800-346-4665

Lincoln Boyhood National Memorial (Lincoln City): 937-4541

Holiday World (Santa Claus): 937-4401

Historic Southern Indiana (preservation group; Evansville): 465-7014

Wyandotte Caves State Recreation Area (Leavenworth): 738-2782

Harrison County Chamber of Commerce (Corydon): 738-2137

Corydon Capital State Historic Site (Corydon): 738-4890

1883 Corydon Scenic Railroad (Corydon): 738-8000

11

The River Road Through History

Angel Mounds State Historic Site to Sulphur Springs

Getting there: From Indianapolis, travel southwest on SR 37 to I-64, then west on I-64 to U.S. 41 south to Evansville. Take I-164 to the Covert Avenue exit. Follow the signs on Stacer Street south to Angel Mounds State Historic Site.

Highlights: explore a prehistoric Indian village; watch boats in the Newburgh locks; view the *Christ of the Ohio* statue; sample Tell City pretzels.

Look out over more than a hundred acres of grassy land bounded by woodland and imagine a thriving prehistoric village. Here and there on the grassy hummocks stood a temple, storerooms, and square and round houses. Protected by a stockade forming an arc over a mile long, Mississippian

99

Indians went about their daily chores—growing corn and other vegetables, gathering plants, preparing food, mending roofs, building canoes, tending children, and fishing from a stream. Walk these paths today and you can picture the thousand or more people who once lived here on a bank of the broad Ohio River.

Begin your journey at Angel Mounds, a site some have called one of the best-preserved Indian prehistoric sites in North America. Assisted by teams of WPA workers, archaeologist Glenn Black found 2.3 million items here between 1939 and 1942. Though much has been learned about the lifestyle of these early people, several of the mounds have not yet been excavated.

In the interpretive center, the gateway to the site, a simulated excavation, well-presented exhibits, and a slide show describe what's been found. With a self-guided tour map in hand, follow pathways around the historic site to see models of early cane-and-daub dwellings, an early log canoe, and the grassy mounds of earth that made this village so distinctive.

Exit Angel Mounds and turn right. Drive east along Pollack Avenue to the end and turn north onto SR 662 toward Newburgh. This riverside highway leads past the Knob Hill Tavern, a pleasant stop for pizza, sandwiches, soups, and salads. Continue east into Newburgh, where the route follows Jennings Street. On the right, you'll see the charming old Homestead Restaurant. This once-thriving town, passed by when major railroads came in, revived briefly during the 1920s with the building of a nearby dam and locks. In the 1970s, after many storefronts had been abandoned, concerned citizens launched Historic Newburgh, Inc., to restore and preserve the town's vintage buildings. A newer dam and locks made the river more navigable and helped prevent seasonal flooding. Since 1983, four square blocks of Newburgh's main-street community have been preserved for the enjoyment of all.

The area has 29 different historic sites, most along Jennings, Water, and State Streets. As you stroll down these old streets, note the signs that provide historic background. One relates a tale of Confederate raiders who took over Newburgh—using fake cannons that resembled stove pipes—without a shot being fired. At the time, the Exchange Hotel, on the southwest corner of Jennings and State Streets, was in use as a hospital for Union troops.

Several intriguing buildings along State Street date from the 1850s, and Newburgh's oldest house, a dirt-floored cottage built by saddle maker Joseph Weis, goes back to 1837. Its framework of rough timbers was put together with wooden pegs; thin trees hold up the roof. The original bricks came in on a flatboat.

In one charming bed and breakfast, guests may read in the library or gather in the living room to enjoy the two fireplaces. For unbeatable relaxation, try out a rocking chair on the covered veranda. A merchant and philanthropist named A. M. Phelps originally built his home in the nineteenth century. From a third-floor cupola, he could watch riverboats ply Ohio River waters. The rooms, still large, have nine-foot windows trimmed with original shutters. The mansion has also retained the wide plank floors Phelps installed himself.

The Kuebler house at 700 Jefferson Street once had an elaborate garden with a lake, a greenhouse, a winery, a cafe, and guest cottages. Between 1889 and 1930, people came by rail from Evansville, getting off at the depot on Water Street to visit Kuebler's Garden and to watch baseball games, horse races, and stage shows in Newburgh.

Drive east on Water Street to SR 662; continue on and you'll meet SR 66. Turn right, drive east, and you'll see the newest dam and locks built at Newburgh. Completed in 1975, this facility cost more than $100 million, and the high-tech operating system has push-button controls. A long blast of a boat whistle followed by a short one signals a boat about to enter the locks. Above these locks on the right bank, just below the overlook, you can sit and watch the boats as the water levels change.

Roughly one mile farther, the Old Stone House perches on a bluff above a wide valley vista. The owners have restored this stately Federal-style place, built on the site of an early frontier stockade.

Continue east on SR 66 through Yankeetown, which was settled by New Englanders. The route crosses Little Pigeon Creek and winds through Spencer County, named for a captain who died leading the Yellow Jacket brigade in the Battle of Tippecanoe.

At SR 45, turn south at the sign for a look at tiny Rockport. This town of 2,590 people is the county's largest and also the seat of government. Actress Florence Henderson grew up here, as did several other notables. SR 45 follows Fifth Street. At Main Street, turn left (east) and take this road downhill to the river's edge. In 1808, the first settlers built cabins at the base of the bluff, calling the village Hanging Rock. Aware of the risks from flood damage and injury by falling rock, they eventually moved the village to the present cliff-top location. Construction of the Newburgh dam has widened the river, reducing the land area formerly occupied by the town. In 1828, Abraham Lincoln left from this port on a flatboat for a river trip to New Orleans.

North of the Lincoln marker, return to Rockport via Second Street and you'll pass the Brown-Kercheval house at 315 South Second Street. Built by a banker, the house was occupied for years by Samuel Kercheval, a manufacturer, publisher, legislator, and mayor, and his wife, Cornelia. The couple entertained many Hoosier notables, including author Meredith Nicholson, who wrote about their hospitality.

Continue on Second Street to Main Street, to the Spencer County Courthouse, a Bedford limestone structure with a stained-glass dome. Abraham Lincoln once gave a speech at this square while campaigning for Henry Clay. During his visit, Lincoln stayed at the Rockport Tavern, an inn at Second and Main Streets. Various buildings in the community have murals or paintings relating to Lincoln.

Drive north to Main Street and go west through the city park to see the Lincoln Pioneer Village. After much research, a historian and other local citizens developed a model village with 11 buildings from the Lincoln era—a church, an inn, a school, an office, and stores. Later, they added more and for several decades the village was a major tourist attraction.

Return to Fifth Street and turn left (north) on SR 45. On the way out of town, you'll notice a drive-in restaurant operating in a renovated railroad car. Turn right (east) onto SR 66, and drive to Grandview, where the county's first permanent settlers, the Ezekiel Ray family, arrived on a raft in 1807. You might enjoy picnicking at the riverside park here in a grove of trees. Note that Abraham Lincoln used the route you've been driving when he brought hoop poles (timber) by oxcart to the river to sell.

Continue east on SR 66 to Ferry Park, at the junction of the Anderson and Ohio Rivers. The Lincolns landed here in 1816 when they first moved to Indiana. The future president also worked here for about a year on a ferry crossing the Anderson River.

Scenic SR 66 continues along the Ohio River. When you reach Camp Koch, a summer camp for handicapped young people, look for a large statue near the camp on Fulton Hill. The *Christ of the Ohio*, 18 feet high, was cast by sculptor Herbert Jogerst from durable, synthetic material.

Drive east on SR 66 through Troy and around the west side of Tell City. The route enters the town on

Twelfth Street. The early Germans and Swiss who settled here platted the town with wide streets named for leaders in government, science, and the arts. After a damaging 1937 flood, the citizens completed the flood wall you'll see protecting Tell City.

Turn right at Jefferson Street and go south for 11 blocks to Main Street. At the corner of Jefferson and Main Streets, the city hall was built in 1896 by officials who hoped it would become the courthouse when the town became the Perry County seat. However, this never happened. Later, a benefactor hired Evansville artist Donald Ingle to make the William Tell sculpture. A copy of a monument beside Lake Lucerne in Switzerland now stands beside the city hall. On Main Street, two blocks south of the city hall, the bakery at the Tell City Pretzel Company has long been a southern Indiana institution. The bakers mix the dough from a secret recipe, then hand twist, glaze, and salt the pretzels before baking them to a tasty crispness.

From Main Street, return to SR 66, past the Patio Steak House. Rebuilt after a 1990 fire, this popular local place is known for its beef and a well-stocked salad bar.

Continue east to Cannelton, where an impressive spire rises from St. Michael's Roman Catholic Church, built in Gothic style. SR 66 enters Cannelton on Seventh Street. An early port community called Coal Haven flourished here in the early 1800s. For more than a century, the Cannelton Cotton Mill was a major industry, but it closed in 1954. Concerned local people have preserved early buildings, and the area between Richardson, Taylor, First, and Madison Streets has become a historic district.

Two miles east of Cannelton on SR 66, you'll come to an overlook for the Cannelton Locks and Dam. The river's navigable channels have been marked with buoys—black on the right, red on the left. The system of dams and locks, built by the U.S. Army Corps of Engineers, minimizes seasonal flooding and forms a series of stepped water levels, higher above each dam. Take in the scene from the visitors' observation building.

Beyond Cannelton, follow the river road east for dramatic climbing turns that drop abruptly down to farmers' stubbled fields. Anyone subject to motion sickness should take a front seat, keep the head level, and gaze at the horizon. Acupressure wrist bands or anti-motion-sickness medication might also be useful for the drive ahead.

The wiggly road north cuts through Hoosier National Forest land and tests the driver's cornering skills. You'll wind through scenic valleys and across German Ridge, to cut once more through fields with grazing cattle. Rocky cliffs topped with forest rise to the left. On the right, you have a broad, peaceful view of the river.

Sulphur Springs, not much to see now, was once a popular health resort. Scenic SR 66 ends at Sulphur Springs, and so does your journey.

For More Information

All numbers are within area code 812.

Evansville Convention and Visitors' Bureau: 800-433-3025

Angel Mounds State Historic Site (Evansville): 853-3956

Knob Hill Tavern (Newburgh): 853-9550

Hoosier National Forest (office; Bedford): 275-5987

Patio Steak House (Tell City): 547-4949

12

Travel Through a River Valley's Past

Versailles to Rising Sun

Getting there: From Indianapolis or Louisville, take I-65 to U.S. 50. Drive east on U.S. 50 to Versailles; the trip begins in Versailles State Park on U.S. 50 east of town.

Highlights: listen to bluegrass music in a wooded setting, stroll a historic main street, or rest while riverboats chug by; visit an old Swiss community, watch a horse-pulling contest, and end the drive beside a scenic creek.

A line of trees along Laughery Creek has all the warm palette colors: cerise, ochre, smoke, flame, and forest green. Splintered rays of sun break behind branches cast in shadow. Stunning in autumn, this is only one of many such scenes in Versailles State Park, background for hikes along sylvan trails, outings in small boats, and relaxing on the lakeshore. The annual Bluegrass Festival at the park features more than a dozen bands playing foot-stomping, clap-happy tunes every October, peak time for fall foliage. Spring in Versailles State Park (local people say "vur sails") is also a favorite season. Hike past flowering trees and patches of wildflowers, or take out a horse from the stable. Begin this drive at the park entrance, swing around the park's woodland roads, and choose a scenic setting for a breakfast picnic.

When you leave the park, turn right (west) on SR 50 across Laughery Creek. From its headwaters near Batesville, the stream rambles through the valleys to join the Ohio River near Aurora. Limestone cliffs flank the road as you enter the bucolic country village of Versailles.

At the intersection, take SR 129 south toward Madison. In sunlight, the fields and forests become golden greens, tans, and earthy browns. The road you travel follows the crest of a ridge above a sweeping valley.

At the junction with SR 62, turn west onto the highway known as Chief White Eye Trail. While settlers encroached on Native American lands, Chief White Eye worked valiantly to keep his tribal people neutral, avoiding battles with whites. The beautiful trail is a fitting memorial.

Continue on SR 62 past a country church. The winding road enters a wooded valley and runs over a rocky creek where water bubbles down a gentle slope. Beyond, bales of hay stand here and there in quiet fields. Behind an abandoned cottage is a ramshackle outhouse. In summer, wildflowers bloom profusely in shades of cream, lavender, and rosy yellow. Stop a moment by a hillside choked with foliage. Without the engine's rumble, you can hear the whistles of hidden birds.

At U.S. 421, turn south and drive four miles into Madison. Descend between dramatic cliffs into the Ohio River valley. Ignore the paved roads and modern signs,

and you could well be rattling down the incline in a stage-coach, glancing at rows of quaint houses that line the sidewalks and stately hillside homes overlooking the wide Ohio. In 1977, the National Trust for Historic Preservation chose Madison and two other U.S. cities for the Main Street Project. Yet years before, Madison had preserved its early architecture, some say because people couldn't afford to tear down old buildings to put up new ones. Visitors today find an appealing blend of period art and function: former residences that have become small inns, cafes in historic buildings, a vintage main street lined with intriguing shops and stores. Although the Scottella Winery never reopened after its fire, the Thomas Family, Lanthier, and Madison Wineries now operate here.

Located at the end of the old Michigan Road, the port city of Madison thrived during the early nineteenth century. By 1816, Madison was the largest town in the new state of Indiana, and by 1830, the population had reached 1,752. Surrounded by hills, Madison has developed over the years on two levels. U.S. 421 enters Madison on Jefferson Street. Follow it south past First Street to reach the Vaughn Street riverside drive. From the bank you'll see a major bridge linking Indiana and Kentucky. A promenade with wooden benches runs along the street and riverside.

Before strolling along Main Street, stop at the visitors' center (301 East Main at Jefferson). Ask for walking-tour maps with background on each historic building. More than two dozen buildings of historic significance invite your exploration. The area also has several small wineries and charming bed-and-breakfast inns. Here are many of the favorites among everything Madison has to offer.

The Broadway Fountain (Broadway and Main Street) has become an icon for Madison's rebirth. The James Lanier Mansion State Historic Site—perhaps Indiana's finest antebellum residence—deserves a visit. The Talbott-Hyatt house has an unusual pioneer garden and an early well. Dr. William Hutching's Office and Hospital has early furnishings and old medical equipment. Madison's Broadway Historic Tavern/ Hotel has been a gathering place since 1859. St. Michael's Roman Catholic Church, the town's second oldest public building, still holds services. And do see Fair Play Fire Company No. 1. Overall, Madison has much to offer without being too touristy or overcrowded. Relax over coffee or enjoy a meal at the Upper Crust.

Madison's special events run from spring through fall. Enjoy a spring garden tour in late April or early May, an early history festival called River Days, a regatta with hydroplane races on the river, the prestigious Chautauqua of the Arts festival, or an autumn home tour in late September.

From Madison take Main Street (SR 56 east) along the Ohio River toward Vevay. The riverside drive soon becomes a literal cliff-hanger, for it clings to a ledge below a rugged rock wall on the left. Wooded hills fill in the middle distance. On the right, absorb the splendid view, as pleasure boats zip past barges churning as if in slow motion through muddy river waters. Set into the hill, the Captain's Quarters, a bed-and-breakfast inn (make reservations ahead), has great views.

Continue on SR 56 and you'll cross Indian Creek just before entering Vevay. Between the highway and the river, note the Ogle Haus Inn, built by a local businessman and philanthropist named Paul Ogle. Ogle's story was one of hometown boy makes good. A music lover and talented saxophone player, Ogle promoted tourism, created jobs in the town, and launched many civic projects as well. Vevay (pronounced "vee vee" by locals) was settled by Swiss immigrants who brought vinifera grape rootstock to the New World along with all their other valuables. After planting the vineyards, it wasn't long before winemakers were turning out 12,000 gallons of wine a year. For a time, the Ohio River was a vital transportation link, and the port town did a brisk business shipping wine and other beverages, tobacco, and farm products. Today, Vevay recognizes its heritage with an annual wine festival.

SR 56 enters Vevay on Main Street, graced here and there with the charming homes of an earlier era. Renovated and well maintained, many are in use as private homes. Before you stroll through the historic district, ask for a map of the 28 vintage nineteenth-century buildings. Several important early buildings still stand in the 300 block of West Main Street, and the heart of downtown Vevay is at Ferry and Main Streets. Stroll around the neighborhood to find several favorites: the home of Edward Eggleston, a novelist and preacher who wrote *The Hoosier Schoolmaster*; the Armstrong Tavern, the oldest building known to have been used as a Masonic Lodge; the E. P. Schenk house, former residence of a businessman who operated a fleet of riverboats; and the Grisard-Sieglitz place, built in 1848.

If you visit Vevay in early summer, the town hosts an annual horse-pull contest at the 4-H fairgrounds. Prizes and trophies go to winners of weight-pulling contests and other competitions—in the best Hoosier rural tradition.

Leaving Vevay, SR 56 east snakes uphill to the top of a bluff and follows a ridge through southeastern Indiana high country. You'll have expansive views on either side and may even notice a man resting in a lawn chair, who often waves at strangers as they pass. Beyond the village known as East Enterprise, you'll spot a road named Lovers' Lane (really). Open the windows as you drive along, and you can tell it's dairy farm country before you even see the pastures, cows, and barns. Down the road, tobacco dries in a shed, wildflowers bloom, and other fields lie fallow.

Continue on SR 56 to Rising Sun, entering the town on (what else?) Main Street. No one quite knows how the town got its name. Some say early travelers first saw the place by the dazzling light of sunrise. The rows of houses along Front Street (edging the river) date from the early 1800s. Stroll past these private homes and enjoy the river view, the park, and the playground. The Rising Sun Seminary on Fourth Street, which opened in 1836 as the Indiana Teachers' Seminary, was the state's first normal school. In quiet Rising Sun, there's not a tourist trap in sight.

Follow SR 56 east from Rising Sun, past renovated older homes with lovely valley views. North of the village, the road crosses Laughery Creek near its confluence with the Ohio River. Laughery once led a band of soldiers along this route, intent on joining George Rogers Clark. Short of rations and carrying limited supplies of ammunition, the men were vulnerable, and even though Laughery led his men heroically, when Indians attacked they were overwhelmed.

Thus, the riverside journey ends, as it began, beside a creek called Laughery.

For More Information

All numbers are within area code 812.

Historic Hoosier Hills (Versailles): 689-6456

Versailles State Park (Versailles): 689-6424

Madison Area Visitors' Center (Madison): 265-2956

Jefferson County Historical Society (Madison): 265-2335

James Lanier Mansion State Historic Site (Madison): 265-3526

Broadway Historic Tavern/Hotel (Madison): 265-2346

Main Street Bed and Breakfast (Madison): 265-3539

The Upper Crust (Madison): 265-6727

Switzerland County Welcome Center (Vevay): 800-HELLO-VV

Captain's Quarters Bed and Breakfast (Vevay): 427-2900

Rising Sun/Ohio County Tourism Bureau (Rising Sun): 438-4591

The Front Parlor (antiques and collectibles; Rising Sun):
   438-3751

Index